A Short Introduction to

Attachment and Attachment Disorder

Second Edition

Colby Pearce

Jessica Kingsley *Publishers*
London and Philadelphia

First edition published in 2009 by Jessica Kingsley Publishers
This second edition first published in 2017
by Jessica Kingsley Publishers
73 Collier Street
London N1 9BE, UK
and
400 Market Street, Suite 400
Philadelphia, PA 19106, USA

www.jkp.com

Library of Congress Cataloging in Publication Data
Pearce, Colby.
 A short introduction to attachment and attachment disorder / Colby Pearce.
   p. cm.
 Includes bibliographical references and index.
 ISBN 978-1-84310-957-0 (pb : alk. paper) 1. Attachment disorder
in children. 2. Attachment behavior in children. I. Title.
 RJ507.A77.P43 2009
 618.92'8588--dc22
                                        2008049609

British Library Cataloguing in Publication Data
A CIP catalogue record for this book is available from the British Library

ISBN 978 1 78592 058 5
eISBN 978 1 78450 315 4

Printed and bound in Great Britain

*To those who believed in me,
so that I might believe in myself.*

ACKNOWLEDGEMENTS

The writer wishes to acknowledge all of the feedback and support he has received from caregivers, professionals and academics from around the world since the publication of the first edition of this book. In particular, the writer would like to acknowledge Mr John Gibson of Secure Attachment Matters Ireland for his valued support and guidance and his collaboration with the writer in the development and implementation of the Triple-A Model of Therapeutic Care, which is a practical extension of the content of this book.

The writer would also like to acknowledge those who made a significant contribution to his early thinking in this field, including Richard Delaney, Dan Hughes and Bruce Perry.

The writer wishes to acknowledge his current interns, Inke Jones and Tara Hearne, for their assistance in collating the referenced material in this edition.

Most importantly, the writer wishes to acknowledge Rebecca, Thomas, Lachlan and Hamish, who remain his secure base.

CONTENTS

Chapter 3

CARE to Promote Attachment Security 70

Chapter 4

Treating Attachment Insecurity and
Disorder: Fundamental Requirements
for Effective Treatment 120

A SHORT INTRODUCTION

Children form significant, lifelong memories of their interactions with adults who enter their lives, including parents, grandparents, aunts and uncles, teachers, sporting coaches and so on. Those memories, and the experiences from which they derive, shape the beliefs children hold with respect to themselves, others and the world in which they live. In doing so, they also shape children's behaviour.

The way adults treat any generation of children shapes the way those children will, in turn, treat the next generation when they are adults. It follows that if we are seeking to create a more gentle, humanistic world we adults need to pause and reflect on how we interact with the current generation of children.

Some time ago I was returning to the Melbourne Central Business District on an overcrowded tram after a day at the Australian Formula One Grand Prix. People were packed into the tram like sardines in a can. Shoulder to shoulder they stood in the aisles, swaying and brushing against each other with every jerk and bump. In this environment of uncomfortable levels of physical closeness to strangers, eye contact is minimal, and conversation, when it exists, is brief and muted.

So it was that I could clearly hear in the carriage behind me a young girl of primary school age initiate a conversation with a complete stranger standing adjacent to her on the tram. The child had apparently noticed that this stranger had spoken with a heavy accent and had summoned the courage to inquire after its origin. The stranger, who I later observed to be young and of European appearance, responded that her accent was Spanish. The child advised the young woman that she was learning Spanish. What followed over almost one hour was a child maintaining an animated and enthusiastic conversation about learning Spanish, to which the young woman responded with acceptance, warmth, patience and corresponding enthusiasm.

As a psychologist who has interacted with children over a long career, I could not help but be impressed, and touched, by the manner in which the young woman engaged with the child. It left me sure that this child would remember fondly the day she interacted with a real-life, Spanish-speaking adult, apart from her teacher. I thought immediately of what might be the legacy of this interaction for the child and what had been the young woman's own experiences of relating to adults when she was a child that had resulted in her warm, accepting and caring manner towards a previously unknown child.

I have included this story here as it reminds me that kindness should be at the heart of all of our endeavours when caring for and relating with children, for their sake and for the sake of generations to come.

Conventional wisdom tells us that if something walks like a duck and talks like a duck, it must be a duck. That is, if it *behaves* like a duck, it must be a duck. Once we have established that something is a duck, our knowledge and experience with ducks tells us what we can expect from the duck and how to relate to it. But what if it looks like a duck but *thinks* like a swan, because it became separated from its mother and father duck and was raised by a swan? Would our expectations regarding its behaviour still be valid? Would we, upon knowing the duck thought like a swan, relate to it as if it were a duck?

I wrote this book because I believe that it is not what children do but why they do it that is crucial to understanding them, relating effectively with them and, where required, intervening successfully with them. This distinction between what children do and why they do it is crucial to the accurate diagnosis of childhood mental disorders and their appropriate and effective treatment. In order to understand why children behave the way they do, one needs to know something of the ways in which they think and the historical circumstances that shaped the way they think.

In this book all who are involved with children in a caregiving role will be able to access information about how a child's early care experiences shape their character. In particular, the reader will be able to access information about the thought processes and preoccupations that give rise to perplexing and challenging behaviour and emotional displays in children who have an early history of inadequate and/or problematic care, as well as strategies to promote more helpful thoughts about self, other and the world. It is anticipated that having a better understanding of why children who have an attachment disorder behave the way they do will assist their caregivers to relate effectively and intervene successfully with them, so that these children may attain the fundamental precursors to a full and satisfying life: believing that the world is a safe place, that they are capable, that they are lovable and deserving of love, and that relationships with others are rewarding.

Within the book I make reference to one gender or other when exemplifying the concepts I am presenting. Unless I state otherwise, I do not intend for the reader to think that the concepts under discussion are gender-specific. Rather, I have generally referred to one gender or the other for ease of reading. Similarly, I would draw the reader's attention to the glossary at the end of this book. The glossary is included to inform and clarify my own interpretation of various terms included in this book, and is reflective of my general endeavour to make the subject matter of the book accessible to the broadest audience possible. As such, it is not intended to be a glossary of professional terms; nor is it intended for professional use only. Rather, I anticipate that the glossary will assist in ensuring that all readers attain a full and satisfying understanding of my experiences and perspectives concerning Attachment and Attachment disorder.

Colby Pearce
June 2016

A TALE OF FOUR MICE

Once upon a time there were four mice.

The first mouse lived in a house that contained, along with furniture and other household goods and possessions, a button and a hole in the wall from which food was delivered. Each time the mouse pressed the button he would receive a tasty morsel of his favourite food. The mouse understood that when he was hungry all he had to do was press the button and food would arrive via the hole. The mouse took great comfort in the predictability of his access to food and only pressed the button when he was hungry.

The second mouse lived in a similar house, also containing a button and a hole in the wall from which food was delivered. Unfortunately, the button in his house was faulty and delivered food on an inconsistent basis when he pressed it, such that he might receive food via the hole on the first, fifth, seventh or even the eleventh time he pressed the button. This mouse learnt that he could not always rely on the button and that he had to press the button many times, even when he was not actually hungry, in order to ensure that he would have food. Even after his button was fixed he found it difficult to stop pressing it frequently and displayed a habit of storing up food.

The third mouse also lived in a similar house, containing a button and a hole in the wall from which food was to be delivered. However, the button in his house did not work at all. He soon learnt that he could not rely on the button and would have to develop other ways of gaining access to food. This belief, and his associated lack of trust in the button, persisted when he moved to a new home with a fully functioning button. He developed unconventional strategies to access food, such as stealing from his neighbour's house.

A fourth mouse was most unfortunate of all. In addition to presses of his button failing to result in the delivery of food, there was a malfunction with his underfloor heating, such that suddenly and without warning the floor would become electrified and he would receive a painful electric shock. In a further twist, the button that was supposed to result in the delivery of food when pressed became the means by which the electrification of the floor could be switched off. This mouse never strayed far from the button and focused intently on it, even when moved to another home where presses of the button consistently resulted in the delivery of food and the floor never became electrified.

CHAPTER 1

UNDERSTANDING ATTACHMENT AND THE INFLUENCE OF PARENTAL CARE

WHAT IS ATTACHMENT?

'Attachment' is a term used to describe the dependency relationship children develop towards their primary caregivers. In ordinary circumstances, an infant's emerging attachment to their primary caregivers begins to show during the latter half of their first year post-birth and develops progressively over the first four years. It is most readily observed when children are sick, injured, tired, anxious, hungry or thirsty, and at reunion after temporary separations.[1, 2]

Although early attachment research focused on the mother–infant dyad, it is now generally accepted that children form multiple attachment relationships. An 'attachment figure' is defined as someone who provides physical and emotional care, has continuity and consistency in the child's life and an emotional investment in the child's life.[3] This can include parents (biological, foster, adopted), grandparents, siblings, aunts and uncles and alternate caregivers (e.g. child-care workers).

Given that children are able to form multiple attachments, the question has been asked as to which attachment relationship is most influential on children's developmental outcomes. The literature provides considerable support for an integrative model of attachment: that is, children's social–emotional development is best predicted by their network of attachment figures rather than by a single attachment relationship *per se*.[4]

WHAT ARE THE ORIGINS OF ATTACHMENT THEORY?

Attachment Theory is the term used when referring to knowledge about attachment. Attachment Theory has developed across more than half a century in association with observations made of children interacting with their caregivers and associated scientific endeavour. It represents an integration of observation and scientific endeavour and reflections about this.

During the 1930s and 1940s psychoanalytically oriented clinicians in the United States and Europe were making observations of the ill effects on personality development of prolonged institutional care and frequent changes of mother-figure during infancy and early childhood. Among them was John Bowlby, a psychiatrist who, prior to receiving his medical training, studied developmental psychology.[5]

At this time the most popular thinking among psychoanalytically oriented clinicians was that infants' goal-directed behaviour was governed by two kinds of drive: primary and secondary. The alleviation of hunger and thirst was thought of as a primary drive and, therefore, as one of the main determining factors in the infants' goal-directed behaviour. As such, infants were considered to form a close bond to their mother *because* she feeds them. Relational aspects of the infant–mother interaction (referred to as 'dependency') were considered to be secondary drives and, therefore, of secondary importance in the infant–mother bond.

Bowlby believed that this did not fit with his observations of institutionalised children. For if it were true, infants of one or two years of age would take readily to whomever fed them – simply being fed would be sufficient for the development of a close bond between infants and their primary caregiver – and this was not what was being observed. It was also inconsistent with emerging scientific evidence from animal studies, including the work of Harry Harlow.[6]

Harlow separated infant rhesus monkeys from their mothers within 6–12 hours of birth and raised them with the aid of two forms of 'mother surrogate'. One was shaped out of wire, whereas the second was shaped from wood and wrapped in towelling to make it soft. Both were warmed by an electric light globe positioned behind the mother surrogate. The main difference was softness. Infant rhesus monkeys were raised with the aid of the two mother surrogates in different combinations. In one combination, infant rhesus monkeys had access to both forms of mother surrogate, but only the wire mother surrogate fed it via an artificial teat from which it could nurse. In another combination, infant rhesus monkeys had access to both mother surrogates but were fed by the cloth-covered mother surrogate only. In both combinations, infant rhesus monkeys demonstrated a clear preference for the soft, cloth-covered mother surrogate, regardless of whether it fed them, spending up to 18 hours per day clinging to the soft mother surrogate. Similarly, when exposed to a fear-evoking situation or stimulus, the infant rhesus monkeys that were raised with both forms of mother surrogate would rush to the soft mother surrogate for comfort, regardless of whether it fed them or not. In addition, Harlow's research demonstrated that those infant rhesus monkeys that spent the early weeks of their life without a soft mother surrogate that they could cling to showed marked disturbance in their emotions and behaviours, which was only ameliorated by the introduction of the soft mother surrogate. Further, all infant rhesus monkeys displayed an apparent attachment to a heated gauze pad placed in the bottom of their cage and became distressed when it was removed for cleaning. Harlow's research clearly demonstrated the pre-eminence of that most basic quality of the caregiving relationship, contact comfort, over physical nourishment in the development of the infant–mother bond.

Consistent with such contemporary challenges to the popular thinking among psychoanalytically oriented clinicians, Bowlby began to formulate a new theory that recognised the primary influence of relational variables in the development of the infant–mother relationship and of the relationship itself on the successful adaptation of the young child to life. Relying heavily on naturalistic observation, but also drawing on the results of scientific research, Bowlby developed what we now know as 'Attachment Theory'.

Among his associates at the Tavistock Clinic in London in the early 1950s was Mary Ainsworth. Her prior interest was in 'security theory', which proposed that infants and young children need to develop a secure dependence on their parents before launching into unfamiliar situations. Through observational studies of mothers and their infants in Uganda and the United States, and her later studies using an experiment called 'the strange situation' (which is discussed later in the chapter)[7], Ainsworth made a significant contribution to the classification of different types of attachment and the identification of the pivotal contribution of the mother's sensitivity to her infant in the development of attachment patterns.

HOW DOES ATTACHMENT DEVELOP?

We like to think that our infant is instantly recognisable to us when they are born and so will we be to them within a short period of time. We experience great pleasure the first time they smile, often thinking that they are smiling at us in recognition and acknowledgement of their shared regard. This is not so far-fetched when we consider that amongst other species in the animal kingdom infants do recognise their mother very shortly after birth via a phenomenon called *imprinting*. As the name implies, some aspect of the mother is 'printed' in the mind of the infant, whether it be the unique pattern of the rump of the mother zebra or the plumage of the mother goose, such that the infant selectively orients to this individual for the satisfaction of its needs over all others. Unfortunately, there is no strong evidence yet to suggest that imprinting occurs in human infants.

Human infants are not born with attachments already made to their primary caregivers. This special relationship emerges over time and through a series of stages. Perhaps the most common model of attachment development, based on the work of John Bowlby[8, 9] and Mary Ainsworth (and associates),[10] and summarised by Richard Delaney,[11] is the one illustrated in Table 1.1.

Table 1.1 Stages of attachment formation

Stage	Time	Observable features
Pre-attachment	Birth to 3 months	The infant orients to the sound of the caregiver's voice, reflexively reaches to be held and tracks the caregiver visually, but smiles reflexively and indiscriminately.
Recognition/discrimination	3–8 months	The infant begins to differentiate between its primary caregivers and others. Smiles are based on recognition, and the infant scans caregivers' faces with excitement. The infant shows distress when caregivers leave the room and smiles at and greets them after brief separations.
Active attachment	8–36 months	During this stage in which the primary attachments are actively developing, the infant demonstrates a clear preference for the primary caregiver or caregivers and a corresponding wariness towards strangers, or 'stranger reaction'. The infant crawls or walks away from their caregiver to explore their environment, though they frequently check back to their caregiver's face, either by returning to their caregiver or visually touching base with him or her. The child explores without anxiety. Once mobile, the child seeks hugs and otherwise seeks temporary reunions with their caregiver before resuming their exploration of their environment. Such temporary reunions are referred to as emotional refuelling.
Partnership	36 months onwards	In this stage attachment solidifies. The child expresses their needs verbally and begins to negotiate conflicts and differences with their caregiver.

WHAT DOES ATTACHMENT LOOK LIKE?

John Bowlby referred to attachment behaviour as any form of activity that results in children accessing and/or maintaining proximity to some other clearly identified individual who they believe is better able to cope with the world.[12] Viewed in this way, attachment behaviour is goal-directed behaviour, the aim of which is the restoration and maintenance of feelings of wellbeing and the satisfaction of needs. Attachment behaviour is most obvious when children are frightened, fatigued or sick and is relieved by comforting and caregiving. At other times the behaviour is less in evidence. Nevertheless, the knowledge that an attachment figure is accessible and responsive provides a strong and pervasive feeling of security and so encourages children to value and continue the relationship and continue to explore and engage with their world. Whilst attachment behaviour is at its most obvious in early childhood, it can be observed throughout the lifespan, especially in emergencies.[13]

Attachment behaviours provide an insight into the nature of children's attachment relationships. They serve to keep the caregiver connected to the child[14] physically ('My caregiver is here for me'), emotionally ('My caregiver understands and shares my feelings') and cognitively ('My caregiver is aware of me'). These behaviours include:[15]

- eye-to-eye gaze
- reaching
- smiling
- signalling or calling to
- pouting
- holding or clinging
- protesting separation
- seeking to be picked up

- following

- sitting with

- searching

- verbal engagement/need expression.

WHAT DIFFERENT TYPES OF ATTACHMENT EXIST?

Attachment patterns were formalised using a procedure known as the Strange Situation.[16] In formal research studies using this procedure, mothers and 12-month-old infants were introduced to a laboratory playroom. An unfamiliar adult joined them shortly thereafter. While the stranger played with the infant, the mother left briefly and then returned. A second separation occurred, during which the infant was left completely alone. Finally, the stranger and then the mother returned. The whole procedure took approximately 20 minutes. The infant's interaction with mother and stranger and its reaction to separations and reunions were studied and the following attachment patterns (also known as *attachment styles*) were identified:

- secure

- insecure–avoidant

- insecure–ambivalent

- disorganised/disoriented.

I will now describe each of these in more detail.

Securely attached infants and children

Securely attached infants[17] exhibit a preference for contact and involvement with their attachment figure, though after an initial period of shyness ('stranger reaction') will feel comfortable enough to engage with strangers towards whom their attachment figure shows no anxiety. Similarly, these children will be content to explore an unfamiliar setting without apparent anxiety (i.e. unreasonable fear) in the presence of their attachment figure. As they develop a sense of 'basic trust'[18] (or perception that the world is a safe place and that relating to others is a satisfying experience) they are content to be left alone with a relative stranger for a short period of time. They exhibit excitement at their attachment figure's return and will top up their emotional cup by initiating a temporary reunion, such as sharing a brief hug, before resuming their confident exploration of their physical and social world. If they are distressed during separation they are readily soothed by their attachment figure when they return to the infant. From the lap of their attachment figure they will orient to their attachment figure's face and also gaze with interest at their surroundings. Although estimates vary, research in Western countries has shown that around 60 per cent of 12–20-month-old infants studied using the Strange Situation might be classified as evidencing an emerging 'secure attachment'.[19]

Insecure–avoidant infants and children

Insecure–avoidant infants[20] appear on the surface to cope best with separations from their attachment figure. Lacking a strong emotional connection to their attachment figure, they will exhibit no clear preference for their attachment figure or a relative stranger. Rather, they appear relatively detached and self-reliant; even self-absorbed. They may avoid or ignore others and rarely initiate affectionate gestures. They appear relatively disinterested in their attachment figure following temporary separations. In their attachment figure's embrace, they are likely to be observed to orient their face away from their attachment figure and fail to cling or return an embrace.

As children, they are more likely to prefer solitary activities and might be described as 'loners'. They appear to have learnt that relating to others is an unsatisfying experience, such as might occur in cases where an attachment figure is typically unresponsive to the child's dependency needs due to being absent or having poor parenting skills or as a result of their own avoidant pattern of relating.

Insecure–ambivalent infants and children

Insecure–ambivalent infants[21] are excessively clingy towards their attachment figure and distressed during separation. Upon reunion with their attachment figure they are likely to be inconsolable and obsessed with the attachment figure and to vacillate between a need for closeness with, and anger at, the attachment figure. An insecure–ambivalent attachment typically develops where infants are inconsistently attended to and soothed by their attachment figure, such as happens when the attachment figure is inconsistently available, physically and emotionally, or where the attachment figure is distressed themselves, thereby amplifying the infant's distress. Typically, insecure–ambivalent infants and children are difficult for the caregiver to settle and exhibit a mixture of dependency and resistance. Insecure–ambivalent children are often perceived to be angry, demanding and needy.

Disorganised/disoriented infants and children

In contrast to the patterns of attachment described above, the defining feature of the disorganised/disoriented infant[22] is that they exhibit no consistent or organised attachment behaviour in response to reunions with their attachment figure. Rather, they display bizarre and contradictory behaviours, such as seeking to be close to their attachment figure but with their gaze averted, approaching the attachment figure only to stop and stare before full physical reunion occurs and alternately engaging with and disengaging from their attachment figure in quick (almost simultaneous) succession. They exhibit incomplete movements and emotional displays, such as reaching to be held or starting to protest only to freeze and/or engage in dazed-like behaviour. In addition, disorganised/disoriented infants exhibit signs of worry in the presence of their attachment figure, such that they might sit on the attachment figure's lap but with eyes averted or might allow the attachment figure to hold them but with their limbs stiff. They might also be observed to avoid or fail to seek out their attachment figure when distressed or frightened and attempt to leave with a stranger rather than their attachment figure. It is likely that these infants have experienced trauma in the relationship with their attachment figure and, at the very least, gross deficiencies in needs provision.

HOW DOES CAREGIVING IMPACT ATTACHMENT? THE CARE MODEL

Consider infants. They are not born with a sophisticated language system. They cannot successfully be reasoned with about who their parents are and, therefore, who they should form an attachment to and who not to. Rather, they form an attachment to the person or persons who they experience to care for them, physically and emotionally, on a continuous basis. A key concept here is what infants *experience*.

In the same way that infants' attachment to their primary attachment figure(s) develops in association with their experience of *who* cares for them, the type of attachment relationship or attachment style is very much dependent on the infants' experience of the care they receive. That is, an infant's attachment style is strongly influenced by the type of care they receive. By care, I refer to how *consistent, accessible, responsive* and *emotionally connected* infants experience their primary attachment figure(s) to be:

- C: Consistency
- A: Accessibility
- R: Responsiveness
- E: Emotional connectedness.

Consistency

In the 1930s psychologist B. F. Skinner developed an apparatus to study the conditions under which our repertoire of behaviour develops. Referred to later as the Skinner Box,[23] the box-like apparatus incorporated a button or lever that electronically controlled the release of food into the box via a feed chute. In his original experiments, Skinner used rats or pigeons, which were placed into the Skinner Box and studied for what they learnt about accessing food by pressing the button or lever.

Skinner hypothesised that behaviours become learnt and integrated into our behavioural repertoire when, in the performance of the behaviour, a desired outcome is achieved. He referred to this desired outcome as *reinforcement*.[24]

Skinner's first task was to determine whether rats and pigeons could learn what was required to access food in a novel environment (i.e. the Skinner Box). He discovered that they could. He then began to study the learning process the animals went through under different reinforcement conditions.[25]

First, Skinner randomly allocated a new group of animals to one of three learning conditions. In condition one the animals received a food reward for each and every press of the button or lever in the Skinner Box. Skinner referred to this condition as *continuous reinforcement* and the animals received food on a consistent basis. The animals in this condition were the quickest to learn that they could access food by pressing the button or lever but pressed the button or lever at a slower rate than the animals in the second condition.

The animals in the second condition received a food reward *inconsistently*, such as on the first, third or even fifth time they pressed the button or lever. It was unpredictable. Skinner referred to this condition as *intermittent reinforcement*. The animals in this condition were slower to learn that they could access food by pressing the button or lever than the animals in the continuous reinforcement condition. In contrast to the animals that received a food reinforcement on a consistent basis, the animals in the intermittent reinforcement condition were more active in pressing the button or lever and spent more time doing so, reflecting an apparent understanding that the button or lever could not always be relied upon for the delivery of food.

The animals in the third condition never received food for pressing the button or lever. These animals did not incorporate pressing the button or lever into their behavioural repertoire, as it never led to a desired outcome. In effect, they never learnt that they could rely on the button or lever for food.

What has all this got to do with human infants, I hear you ask? Well, what Skinner demonstrated in his experiments using the Skinner Box is that the optimal condition for learning is one where an action is *consistently* followed by a desired outcome. That is, what human infants learn about how dependable their attachment figures are for satisfaction of their needs is dependent on how consistently they receive a satisfying, caregiving response to their cues and signals.

Accessibility

'Accessibility' means that the parent is present and available, physically and emotionally, to the infant and child.[26] Harlow's monkeys fared relatively better when they had reliable access to a warm mother surrogate that offered them contact comfort. Having access to this important source of needs provision appeared to play an important role in buffering against the emotionally harmful and behaviourally restricting effects of stressful situations. The same is true of human infants who have yet to learn that their attachment figure continues to exist and be accessible when they do not have direct sensory experience of them.

To fully appreciate the importance of accessibility it is helpful to consider the concepts of 'object constancy' and 'object permanence'.[27, 28] In the early part of their first year, infants appear to believe that the only things that exist are what they can see, hear, smell, touch or taste at that moment. When something is removed from their sensory experience, it is as if it ceases to exist. When the same object is re-presented to the infants they react as if it is the first time they have ever seen it. This may, in part, explain an infant's distress when a warm and interactive carer leaves the room and their interest in (but not necessarily recognition of) the caregiver who returns to the infant. As the first year progresses, infants increasingly recognise stable properties or characteristics of persons and objects with whom they interact on a continuous and consistent basis (object constancy). That is, infants increasingly recognise continuously existing people and objects based on the continuity and consistency of the infant's experience of them. Certain people and objects become familiar aspects of the infant's world with stable and predictable characteristics and qualities. Most often, this is reassuring to infants, as it represents an emerging capacity to perceive their world as consistent and predictable. Other people and objects are less predictable or have predictable characteristics that invoke distress in infants.

Hand in hand with the concept of 'object constancy' is the related concept of 'object permanence'. In association with the process by which infants recognise certain people and objects as having stable and recognisable properties based on their continuous experience of them, infants develop the capacity to form a mental picture of an object or person that is independent of their direct sensory experience of the person or object. This further reinforces the infant's sense of the continuous existence of the person or object independent of sensory experience of them ('object permanence'). This can be a source of comfort and reassurance to infants, allow them to explore their physical world without anxiety and promote their tolerance of separations. It also has wide and lasting implications in terms of how infants relate to people and objects with whom they come into contact through their exploration and experience.

In order for infants and small children to fully develop a belief in there being a person (or persons) who satisfies their needs and helps them cope with the world, that person (or persons) needs to be a continuous and consistent feature of the infant's life; that is, accessible to them.

Responsiveness

Remember the tale of four mice at the beginning of this book? The tale of the fourth mouse reflects further experiments conducted by Skinner in which animals placed in the Skinner Box were subjected to painful electric current that could only be turned off by pressing the lever. Skinner observed that the animals learnt that they could switch off the electrical current in this way, usually by jumping around until they accidently pressed the lever. In much the same way, in usual circumstances, infants learn about the extent to which they can depend on their caregivers to alleviate their distress by way of the response of their caregiver to the infant's distress.

Responsiveness refers to a process by which the attachment figures sensitively, accurately and directly address the needs of the infant.[29] Responsiveness involves the attachment figure observing the infant, the context and the infant's signals, and responding to the infant's needs with understanding. Consistency is an important determinant of the infant's experience of the responsiveness of their attachment figures. Responsiveness plays an important role in shaping the infant's mental representation of what a caregiver is and what can be expected of a caregiver. Consistency, accessibility and responsiveness are interrelated aspects of the infant's experience of CARE. The infant's experience that needs are consistently understood by an accessible attachment figure promotes feelings of wellbeing and dependency on the attachment figure. Experiences of understanding that arise under conditions of parental responsiveness promote experiences of self-worth and wellbeing that act as a powerful buffer against distress that can arise in conditions of adversity.

Emotional connectedness

The fourth aspect of the infant's experience of CARE that plays an influential role in the development of attachment relationships and attachment style relates to the infant's experience of emotional connectedness to their attachment figures. This is commonly referred to in the attachment literature as *affective attunement* and describes the process by which attachment figures tune in to the expressed emotion of the infant and reflect the same or a very similar emotion back to the infant. This connection to the infant's emotional experience is communicated by attachment figures through tone of voice, facial expression and gesture.

It is readily observed during playful interactions and when the infant is distressed. This shared emotional experience is not merely pretended by the attachment figure. Rather, through tuning in to the emotions of the infant the attachment figure experiences an instinctive and congruent emotional response; much like when you cannot help laughing at the laughing baby video or tearing up in response to distress in a loved one. That these episodes of emotional union between infant and attachment figure(s) occur is supported by research that tracked the heart-rate curves of mothers and infants during play and found that they parallel each other.[30] Heart-rate is considered to be a sign of physiological arousal and changes in arousal are a key component of emotional experience.[31] Affective attunement is not considered a one-way process, as even very young infants tune in to the expressed emotion of the attachment figure. This is vividly illustrated in the so-called 'still-face experiments',[32] whereby, after a short period of playful interaction with their five-month old baby, mothers were instructed to adopt a 'dead-pan' expression. The infants immediately recognised this change and were distressed by it, only for their distress to be relieved a short time later when the mother tuned in to their distress, thereby re-establishing a connection, and returned to happy, playful interaction.

Through repeated attunement experiences, children's emotions are validated and regulated through the responsiveness of the caregiver, thus promoting children's experience and perception of emotional connectedness with others and facilitating the safe exploration of a range of emotions, emotional self-awareness and, later, a capacity for empathy.

As mentioned earlier, the type of attachment infants form to their primary attachment figures is strongly influenced by their experiences of CARE. Securely attached infants have experienced their primary attachment figures as consistent and as consistently accessible, responsive and emotionally connected. Insecure–avoidant infants are most likely to have experienced their primary attachment figures as inconsistent, distant, unresponsive and emotionally unavailable. Insecure–ambivalent infants are most likely to have experienced their primary attachment figures as inconsistent, inconsistently accessible and responsive and overly reactive to the infant's distress. Disorganised infants are most likely to have experienced their primary attachment figures as inconsistent, inaccessible, unresponsive, emotionally disengaged and the source of fear and distress.

Factors that impact on the CARE of infants are shown in Table 1.2.

Table 1.2 Parenting factors that impact on CARE

Positive factors	Negative factors
Good parental role models	Parental mental-health problems
Parenting experience	Parental substance abuse
Positive attitude to parenting/ children	Domestic violence
Capacity to identify with others/ empathy	Poor parenting ability/ knowledge
Secure attachment as a child	Insecure attachment as a child

WHY IS ATTACHMENT IMPORTANT?

Central to Attachment Theory is the idea that there is a survival advantage for infants by maintaining closeness to adults and, thus, protection and access to needs-provision. Because the relational tie infants form with their attachment figures has aided survival of the species, early Attachment theorists considered that attachment has been selected through evolutionary processes as a universal aspect of human activity.[33]

According to Attachment Theorists, attachment relationships play a key role in:

- development
- concept of self
- relatedness with others
- resilience to adversity.

Development

An infant's attachment style impacts every aspect of their development. Consider four one-year-old infants in an unfamiliar situation. One is developing a *'secure attachment'*, two infants have *'insecure attachments'* and the fourth has a *'disorganised attachment'*. The secure infant will move away from his attachment figure in order to explore his physical and social world. From time to time he will resume close proximity to his attachment figure before moving away again. Increasingly, he will merely orient visually to his attachment figure and vocalise to her. All the while he is exploring, experiencing and learning about his physical, emotional and social worlds. His motor and cognitive development is stimulated through movement and play. His social and language development is stimulated through interactions with others. His emotional development is stimulated through diverse experiences, including shared emotional experiences with others.

In contrast, one of the insecure infants is clingy and obsessed with his attachment figure, and the other appears disengaged from his attachment figure and others. One seeks to be held all the time and protests at being placed on the floor. He is anxious and requires constant reassurance. His preoccupation with his attachment figure limits his experiences, his exploration and his play and, hence, all aspects of his development. The other infant appears relatively disinterested in his attachment figure and others. He appears relatively content, though his exploration and play are limited by the anxiety evoked in the novel situation and his having learnt that he cannot depend on his attachment figure for the restoration of feelings of wellbeing. His anxiety reduces the likelihood of exploration, thereby also impacting adversely on all aspects of his development.

The fourth infant displays an apparent interest in his surroundings, approaching objects and persons, including his attachment figure. However, he appears unable or unwilling to carry through his apparent intentions, frequently stopping and staring in a dazed manner. He appears restless, distractible and incapable of sustaining interaction with any one person or activity, thus limiting his experience and opportunities for learning.

Development unfolds in a use-dependent manner; that is, the young child learns about important aspects of their physical, emotional and social worlds, and masters various developmental tasks (e.g. crawling, walking, grasping, talking, playing, socialising), through experience, exploration and play. Experience, exploration and play are directly influenced by the extent to which the child feels safe and secure. Feelings of safety and security are directly influenced by the type of attachment the child experiences with their attachment figure(s). Hence, attachment plays an important role in development.

Concept of self

The nature of children's attachment and attachment relationships will contribute to their concept of self. In association with their experiences of good CARE, securely attached infants perceive themselves to be worthy, deserving and competent. Where CARE has been compromised and an insecure or disorganised attachment style has developed, children are less likely to maintain a healthy perception of their worth and deservedness. A child's sense of their worth has far-reaching implications for how they approach life and relationships, including (but not limited to) their approach to schooling and their aspirations for themselves.

Relatedness with others

In an earlier section I described how infants develop a mental representation or template of what an adult in a caregiving role is and what can be expected of them based on their experience of CARE. As a result of good CARE, infants develop a basic trust[34] that the world is a safe place, and relating to others is a satisfying experience. Importantly, as a result of their experience of emotional connectedness with the primary attachment figure(s), children explore and integrate a range of emotions and through shared emotional experiences develop the foundations of a capacity for empathy. Through their efforts to please their attachment figures and avoid displeasing them, children develop an understanding and acceptance of social rules and learn to restrict their impulses to engage in behaviour and emotional displays that are not socially accepted and that compromise the quality of the child's interactions with others. Children's behaviour and emotions become regulated by a concern for maintaining positive and loving relationships with their attachment figure(s), thus establishing the foundations for a life of lawfulness, positive relationships with others and successful parenting of their own children. Where CARE is compromised, aspects of the infant's learning about their relatedness to others is impacted in some way. This will be addressed in the next chapter.

Resilience to adversity

In my 2011 publication *A Short Introduction to Promoting Resilience in Children* I describe the key role that attachment plays in the development of an individual's capacity to take risks, accept challenges and bounce back from frustration and failure. I particularly focus on the role attachment plays in the development of ideas about one's sense of safety, worth and deservedness and associated ideas about the extent to which an individual perceives that they can rely on the support of others when adversity occurs. As a result of good CARE, securely attached children hold positive beliefs about their competency and worth, the sensitivity and responsiveness of others and the safety and providence of their world. As a result, they are more likely to hold and maintain positive beliefs in the face of adversity, to accept challenges and to cope with failure. They are more likely to think realistically about their abilities and to confidently explore their world without the debilitating and restricting effects of worries about competence, safety and accessibility of caring adults. Through confident exploration of their world and acceptance of risks and challenges, securely attached children are more likely to experience mastery, thereby reinforcing their sense of worth and competence.

If they do not succeed, a secure child retains a sense of their own competence and deservedness of positive outcomes and positive expectations of social support that promotes persistence in their endeavours. A secure attachment style prepares a child for a full and satisfying life, unencumbered by worries about worthiness and the support of others.

CHAPTER SUMMARY

- Attachment is a term used to describe the dependency relationship a child develops towards his or her primary caregivers.

- An attachment figure is defined as someone who provides physical and emotional care, has continuity and consistency in the child's life and has an emotional investment in the child's life.[35]

- A child can have more than one attachment figure (e.g. parents and grandparents), each of whom influence the child's expectations and beliefs about themselves and others. The primary attachment figures, however, are the people who are the main source of needs provision to the child and the people with whom the child experiences the closest emotional ties.

- Attachment Theory developed in recognition of the importance of relationship variables to the caregiver–infant bond and the development and emotional wellbeing of the infant.

- Attachment develops over time and through a series of stages.

- Caregiving influences quality and type of attachment, including whether a child's attachment is secure, insecure–avoidant, insecure–ambivalent or disorganised/disoriented.

- An infant's attachment style varies according to the dimensions of CARE they have received from their primary attachment figure(s): Consistency of CARE, Accessibility of attachment figure(s), Responsiveness of attachment figure(s) and Emotional Connectedness of attachment figure(s).

- Attachment influences the young child's development, their relatedness with others, their concept of self and their resilience to adversity.

MATTHEW'S STORY

Matthew's case is fictional. It is included here and at the end of each chapter hereafter in order to illustrate important aspects of how an attachment disorder develops, what distinguishes it from other childhood mental disorders and normal behaviour in children, and the parenting and treatment requirements of children who have an attachment disorder. It is not intended to be a benchmark against which all children suspected of having an attachment disorder can be compared. Though it tells the story of a child who has come to the attention of child-protection authorities, his presentation, care and intervention requirements are also applicable to adopted children who were initially cared for in institutional care environments and traumatised children being raised by kin or in residential care environments. It should be noted that, though no disorder should be diagnosed on the basis of observable behaviour alone, attachment disorders do have features that distinguish them from other disorders of childhood and adolescence, and children who have an attachment disorder are distinguishable from other children. The distinguishing features of children who have an attachment disorder will be described in Chapter 2. Though it is written from the perspective of a clinician working with Matthew, it is intended to be reflective of the experiences of child-protection workers, foster, adoptive and kinship caregivers and others (including residential care workers and teachers) who are responsible for the care and protection of children like Matthew.

Matthew came to the attention of child-protection authorities when he was five months of age. Police had been repeatedly called out to Matthew's home to respond to domestic disputes. On one occasion they determined that neither parent was in a fit state to care for an infant, and child-protection authorities were notified. Matthew was removed from the care of his parents and placed in emergency foster-care accommodation. The next day his parents consented to his ongoing temporary placement in foster care while further investigations into his circumstances were conducted. During these investigations it was discovered that Matthew had bruising to his legs and buttocks that appeared to have been inflicted by another person and for which his parents could not offer an adequate explanation. In addition, drug- and alcohol-fuelled domestic violence was identified to be a recurrent feature of the relationship between Matthew's mother and father. Further assessment revealed that both parents had chaotic care histories themselves, limited social support and mental-health problems.

Matthew's initial foster carer reported that Matthew exhibited an exaggerated startle response but cried briefly and rarely. He was not demanding and did not appear to miss his mother and father. He tended to be floppy in the carer's embrace and did not cling. She commented that he was an unusually easy baby to care for, except after family access.

Family access was initially scheduled to occur three times per week for two hours on the erroneous grounds that this was required to preserve the attachment between Matthew and his parents.[36] Matthew was a crowd favourite at the child-protection office. Not only did his blond hair and blue eyes make him cute, he also did not appear to mind being passed from staff member to staff member. In fact, he was perceived to be a friendly baby as he appeared always to be gazing at others, no matter which child-protection worker was holding him. However, when Matthew was taken into the access room to meet his parents there was an immediate transformation in his behaviour. He cried when passed from a child-protection worker to either parent. He fretted and was difficult for either parent to settle, though he settled readily when handed back to the access supervisor. While being held by his parents, he maintained an averted gaze and at times appeared glassy eyed and rigid, particularly when his parents bickered with each other. He became calm again after access and typically fell asleep while being transported back to his foster placement. However, his foster carer reported that he was restless and unsettled for the remainder of the day.

After three months a decision was made that Matthew should remain in foster care for up to 12 months while his parents engaged with services regarding their drug and alcohol misuse, domestic violence, mental-health problems and deficits in their parenting knowledge. Access was reduced to once per week on the grounds that it unsettled Matthew and that there were not the resources to maintain a thrice-weekly access regime anyway. By the time he was 12 months old Matthew had changed placement three times; the first time because the foster carer only provided emergency care; the second time because the foster carer unexpectedly became ill; and a third time because the placement was only intended to be temporary while a suitable longer-term foster carer was identified. His fourth foster carer reported that, at 12 months of age, Matthew remained an unusually easy child to care for, except in the 12 hours after access with his parents. At access times he was unsettled at separation from his foster carer in order to be transported to the child-protection office, appeared content when being fussed over by child-protection workers at their office but continued to display unusual behaviours in the presence of his parents. Upon entering the access room at the office he would orient to his parents, smile and begin to move towards them, before stopping, orienting away and seeking to re-engage with the access supervisor. Thereafter, throughout the remainder of each access period it was as if he preferred the access supervisor to his parents. Though he did not protest at being held and fussed over by his parents, he continued to orient his face away while on their lap or in their embrace.

CHAPTER **2**

A SHORT INTRODUCTION TO ATTACHMENT DISORDER

WHAT IS ATTACHMENT DISORDER?

Over the last three decades, the term 'attachment disorder' has entered into common usage among professionals and carers who interact with children who display markedly disturbed and developmentally inappropriate relatedness to others. With greater awareness of the consequences of attachment disruption has come endeavours to develop interventions for children who have an attachment disorder and support for those who care for them. In any such endeavour it is important that the children involved are representative of the condition. This allows for the development of specific interventions that can be tested for their effectiveness without the potentially confounding influence of children who do not have the condition being included in the recipient client group. In this chapter I will present an overview of what an attachment disorder is, what it looks like and when to consider an attachment disorder diagnosis.

In the fifth and latest edition of the Diagnostic and Statistical Manual of Mental Disorders (DSM-5)[37] two diagnoses are relevant to the discussion of what an attachment disorder is, what it looks like and when the diagnosis should be used. The first diagnosis is Reactive Attachment Disorder (RAD). RAD might be considered when children show limited dependency on others for comfort, support, protection and nurturance, and limited response to comfort from an adult in a caregiving role. That is, these children are observed to be inhibited, emotionally withdrawn and inordinately self-reliant. Children with RAD must also show disturbances of emotion and emotional responsiveness to others. They are prone to unexplained irritability, sadness and fear, including during nonthreatening interactions with adult caregivers, and are not readily comforted by adult caregivers.

A second diagnosis, Disinhibited Social Engagement Disorder (DSED), is also relevant to any discussion of attachment disorders. DSED might be considered when a child displays culturally inappropriate, overly familiar behaviour with relative strangers. They may display reduced or absent reticence to engage or even go off with adults who are not known to them, be overly familiar in their verbal and physical behaviours towards adults with whom they have previously had no contact, and they may display reduced or absent checking back with their known adult caregiver, including in unfamiliar situations. Whereas children with RAD appear to avoid dependency on others, children with DSED appear to treat everyone as if they are a potential source of care.

Notwithstanding the differences in the presentation of children that might be diagnosed with either of these disorders, there is a common feature. The condition is understood to have arisen as a result of grossly deficient care, as evidenced by either the persistent absence of a caregiver response to the infant's basic needs for comfort, stimulation and affection, or where there is not the opportunity for the development of stable, selective attachments, such as occurs in rotational care environments and institutional care or where there are repeated changes in foster care placement. That is, both groups of children have experienced gross deficits in CARE, as described in Chapter 1, during the period of their lives where they are developing their first attachments: infancy and early childhood (0–4 years). The authors of the DSM-5 urge caution when diagnosing RAD, in particular, for a child aged more than five years, citing a lack of adequate description of how the condition presents in older children and adolescents. While I applaud adopting a cautious approach to diagnosis, I consider that it is possible to develop a picture of how older children who might be diagnosed with RAD or DSED present, and how to promote their recovery from these conditions, by considering the lasting effects of gross and persistent deficits in CARE.

CARE AND ATTACHMENT

As presented in Chapter 1, CARE influences the type of attachment, or attachment style, a child develops. Deficits in CARE often result in insecure and disorganised/disoriented attachment styles. It follows that children who might be diagnosed with an attachment disorder are likely to have an insecure or disorganised/disoriented attachment style, if they have any form of attachment to a caregiver at all. As insecure and disorganised/disoriented attachment styles have adverse effects on development, the development of the child who has an attachment disorder is compromised. Restricted range of emotion, limited expressive language abilities, impaired thinking and planning and deficits in fine and gross motor coordination and control are common aspects of the presentation of children who have an attachment disorder.

The way a child relates to themselves, others and their world is also impacted by attachment formation and attachment style. As a result of their attachment experiences, and through relating to their primary attachment figures, children develop a sense of themselves, who and what others represent and what relating to them is like and what interacting with the world is like. This sense of themselves, others and the world is represented in a set of interrelated beliefs that are commonly referred to as attachment representations or internal working models.[38, 39, 40, 41, 42] These beliefs are typically unconscious, in that the child generally does not and cannot articulate them, but they reflect the way in which the child presents – what they look like and what appears to *drive* them. Among older children they can be raised to conscious awareness in psychotherapy, which I will elaborate on in Chapter 4.

Figure 2.1 illustrates attachment representations associated with attachment security/disorder and representations of self and other. I have deliberately used two globes to represent the idea that attachment representations reflect a child's worldview. The globes are overlapping to represent my observation that worldviews are rarely, if ever, entirely positive or entirely negative. Rather, there is at least a little bit of the other worldview in all of us. There are bi-directional arrows where the globes overlap. I have included these to represent my observation that people, including children who have an attachment disorder, move back and forth between these two worldviews, depending on what their predominate experience is at a given time. The difference, from one person to another, is which set of attachment representations predominate and exert the greatest influence over the way in which the person interacts with herself, others and her world.

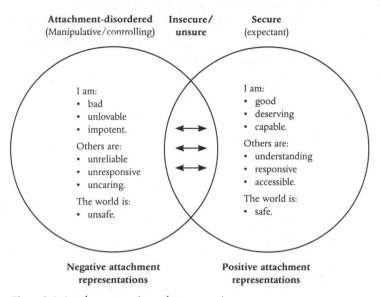

Figure 2.1 Attachment security and representations
regarding self, other and world

The securely attached child develops mostly positive representations of herself, her attachment figure and her world. In association with her experience of CARE, she perceives herself as worthwhile/wanted ('I am loved'), safe ('My attachment figure protects me from harmful experiences') and capable ('My attachment figure is encouraging and supportive of my efforts').[43] She develops basic trust,[44] an expectation that the world will generally be safe and that close relationships will be satisfying. That is, she expects that other caring adults will act much the same as her primary attachment figures do. The securely attached child has a well-formed sense of right and wrong that grows out of her desire to please her attachment figures and avoid displeasing them. The securely attached child attends to her body's cues regarding her needs (e.g. the need for comfort, physical sustenance or to go to the bathroom), exhibits a range of genuine emotion, and has the ability to identify and express her needs through spoken language.[45] Though elements of negative attachment representations are sometimes in evidence, positive attachment representations predominate (Figure 2.2).

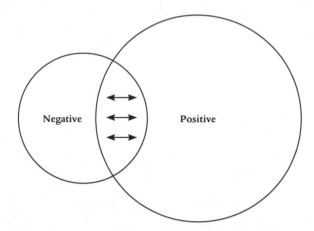

Figure 2.2 Attachment representations of the securely attached child

In contrast, the attachment representations of children who have an attachment disorder are essentially negative. In association with gross and persistent deficiencies in their experience of CARE, the child who has an attachment disorder views himself as worthless ('I am bad, unlovable and undeserving'), unsafe ('My attachment figure will not protect me from traumatic experiences') and impotent ('It is impossible to get my attachment figure to respond consistently to my needs').[46, 47] He views his primary attachment figures as unreliable, unresponsive, rejecting and threatening.[48] He expects intimate relationships to be undependable and ultimately frustrating of his needs.[49] He uses manipulation as a means to make his caregivers and others (e.g. teachers) behave in predictable ways in order to promote feelings of security. Though elements of positive attachment representations are sometimes in evidence, negative attachment representations predominate (Figure 2.3).

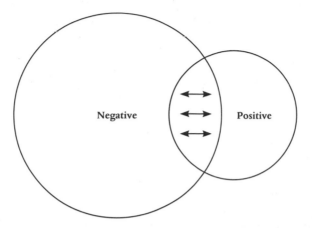

Figure 2.3 Attachment representations of children
who have an attachment disorder

Disordered attachment representations are thought to develop
when normal attachment behaviours fail to consistently elicit
CARE, as may occur where there is limited accessibility to
a consistent caring adult (e.g. in an orphanage), where the
caregiver lacks basic parenting skills and knowledge or in
cases of parental mental disorder, substance abuse or domestic
violence.[50] Under these circumstances the infant experiences
heightened states of fear and distress, for which they are
inconsistently soothed, relaxed or comforted. Fear and distress
are represented physiologically, as chronic elevation in the
level of activation of the child's nervous system (also known
as *arousal*). What this looks like, and how this contributes to
our description of children who have an attachment disorder,
is presented in the next section.

CARE AND AROUSAL

Gross deficiencies in CARE, such that it meets the DSM-5
criteria for diagnosis of RAD and DSED, occur where there
are deficiencies in the person or persons doing the caregiving,

in the care environment or in the care arrangements. Gross deficiencies in the person occur when the infant's main caregiver is unable or unwilling to provide even a basic level of care due to mental or psychological incapacity or lifestyle issues (such as drug and alcohol abuse) that impair their functioning and responsiveness to the infant's need for comfort, stimulation and nurturance. Gross deficiencies in the environment occur when the nature of the care environment (e.g. congregate care environments with high child-to-carer ratios) leave the child in prolonged or persistent reduced access to an adult caregiver who alleviates their distress and attends to their other needs. Gross deficiencies in care arrangements occur when the infant lacks experience of a consistent adult who is consistently accessible, responsive and emotionally connected to the infant, such as occurs when there are frequent changes of caregiver.

The common-usage term for such gross deficiencies in CARE is *neglect*. Where gross deficiencies in CARE occur, infants are also vulnerable to being hurt by adults who cannot or will not regulate their emotions and behaviours according to community standards of what is acceptable. This is *abuse*. Persistent and unremitting neglect (and abuse) in these forms, such that the infant is denied sustained periods of safety, security and happiness, results in prolonged physical and emotional *distress*. As this time of deficient CARE and heightened distress occurs at a time of rapid growth and development, it shapes growth and development. As it is persistent, as opposed to a single incident, it is *complex*. Seen in this way, contemporary endeavours in the field of *Complex Developmental Trauma* offer further understanding of how children with attachment disorders present and how to promote their recovery.

A consequence of the persistent and inconsistently relieved distress arising under conditions of neglectful (and abusive) CARE is persistently elevated *arousal*. Arousal refers to the level of activation of a person's nervous system. One way of thinking of arousal is to consider the petrol engine in your car. Your engine has an idle speed (which reflects the number of turns of the engine's crankshaft per minute or RPM), which is usually maintained without any depression of the car's accelerator. It has a comfortable running speed, which is usually achieved with a slight depression of the accelerator. There is a speed at which the engine becomes overworked and is at risk of blowing up. This is commonly referred to as the red-line point.

A person's nervous system has an idle speed, a comfortable running speed and a speed at which it becomes overwhelmed and is at risk of blowing up. While the speed of the motor increases with increased depression of the accelerator, a person's nervous system runs faster in response to internal (thoughts and sensations) and external (sights, sounds, smells, touches and tastes) stimuli that register on a person's nervous system.

While every person's nervous system, in effect, has an idle speed, a comfortable running speed and a red-line speed, there are differences between people as to where the idle speed is set with respect to the red-line speed.

For many people, the idle speed is low and the red-line speed is high, meaning that they can tolerate a good deal of stimulation before they blow up. For other people, their idle speed is set too high and too close to the red-line speed, such that they are at chronic risk of blowing up. Such is the outcome of persistent deficiencies in CARE and Complex Developmental Trauma that characterise the early experience of the child who has an attachment disorder.

Our bodies have evolved a range of protective mechanisms to manage situations and circumstances under which we experience heightened distress and/or feel threatened. One of these protective mechanisms is that the body reduces blood flow to the peripheral vascular system and increases blood flow to the inner parts of the body; hence the unusual sensation we get in our tummy when we are anxious and the feeling of light-headedness when we experience heightened states of emotion. It is speculated that this protective measure was passed on through generations of humans, as it aided in survival from a cave lion attack or an assault by neighbours armed with spears, thereby increasing the opportunity for procreation and passing on genetic material.

This is all well and good, until you consider the infant who is in a persistent state of unrelieved distress as a result of gross deficiencies in CARE. A very big problem is that certain aspects of their brains are under-developed, whereas others are developing rapidly. Many who are interested in this area have seen the confronting images of the brain of a neglected three-year-old alongside that of a three-year-old who is presumed to have experienced normal CARE.[51] The brain of the neglected child is comparatively small and less well developed, particularly in its outer structures. Though this comparison is controversial, it does highlight the consequence of increased blood flow to the inner parts of the brain and reduced blood flow to the outer structures of the brain during this formative period of growth and development.

Blood flow oxygenates tissue, thereby promoting growth. Among infants who have experienced persistent and unrelieved distress in association with gross deficiencies in CARE, the inner structures of the brain receive more blood flow than the outer structures. The inner structures are comparatively well developed, as compared with the outer structures. This has clear implications for the ongoing functioning of the child, their development and our understanding of the presentation of the child who has an attachment disorder.

Children who have an attachment disorder are chronically under the influence of the inner structures of their brain and the functions they serve. This arises because the outer structures of their brain, that is those structures that are responsible for reflective thinking, problem-solving and effective action, are less well developed, such that they are more easily overwhelmed by the demands placed on them in their day-to-day lives. Development that has occurred in these regions has occurred under conditions of heightened distress and perception of threat, which has shaped their learning and contributed to an outcome whereby they are sensitised to threat. They are constantly on alert and chronically susceptible to hyperarousal. The effect of this is two-fold:

- chronic activation of the inner structures of the brain and behaviours associated with the fight-flight-freeze response

- ongoing deficits in performance and learning.

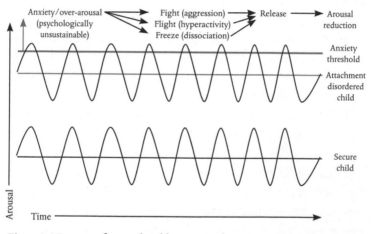

Figure 2.4 Patterns of arousal and hyperarousal

Figure 2.4 shows how the chronic susceptibility to hyperarousal of children who have an attachment disorder adversely impacts their behaviour and emotions. In contrast to securely attached children, who have a slower idle speed and whose typical fluctuations in arousal rarely reach the red-line point (anxiety threshold), the chronically hyperaroused child who has an attachment disorder, by virtue of their faster idle speed,[52] exists much closer to this threshold. Stimuli and events that have a comparatively minor impact on the secure child can much more readily push the child who has an attachment disorder past the red-line point, whereupon they seek to reduce arousal and restore what passes for them as feelings of wellbeing through controlling, aggressive and destructive behaviours (fight), running and hiding behaviour (flight) and/or reduced responsiveness to the environment (freeze). This fight-flight-freeze response is considered to have been naturally selected through evolution in order to achieve feelings of safety and wellbeing in the face of threats to the organism, much as attachment is thought to have developed through evolutionary processes. It is an instinctive survival response that is activated when a person is feeling increasingly under threat and is under the influence of the inner brain structures. It is non-volitional, as are the behaviours exhibited by the child when under the influence of the fight-flight-freeze response. That is, the controlling, aggressive, destructive, hyperactive and disengaged behaviours exhibited by children who have an attachment disorder represent their body's attempt to address their feelings of being threatened and restore feelings of interpersonal safety. Seen in this way, one can readily see that the prevailing imperative for adults interacting with children who have an attachment disorder is to reduce arousal through the provision of good CARE and the promotion of safe environments. Arousal management is a key aspect of the care and management of children who have an attachment disorder.

Figure 2.5 illustrates the relationship between stress/arousal and performance/learning. A certain degree of arousal (i.e. brain activity, alertness, attention) is necessary for peak performance and learning. However, there is a threshold beyond which performance and learning decline in association with increases in stress and arousal. This is best illustrated by the example of walking a balance beam. Most people can successfully negotiate their way across a balance beam raised off the ground by a house brick at each end. They consider themselves able and have no concerns for their physical safety. However, place the same balance beam between the windows of two adjacent buildings ten stories off the ground and most people would experience heightened states of anxiety and hyperarousal. They would be overwhelmed by fear regarding their physical safety. They would doubt their ability to negotiate the balance beam successfully. They would lose coordination and their performance would suffer accordingly, thus confirming their fear that they will be harmed and exacerbating their anxiety and hyperarousal. In association with their own chronically hyperaroused state, the performance and learning of children who have an attachment disorder is similarly compromised. They struggle at school and, in association with these struggles, they doubt their worth and deservedness. They have fewer mastery experiences, such that they are reluctant to try new things and avoid challenges. Though they have survived much, they do not cope or respond well to adversity and do not bounce back readily from perceived or actual failures, such that they might be described as having poor resilience.

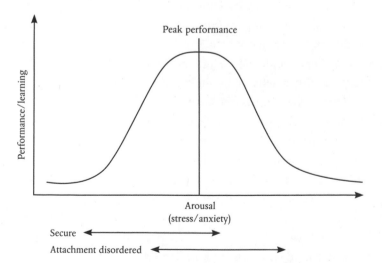

Figure 2.5 Relationship between arousal and performance/learning

CARE AND LEARNING

In Chapter 1, I introduced the work of B. F. Skinner and his contribution to our understanding of the conditions under which optimal learning occurs. I presented information about how the optimal condition for learning is that in which a desired outcome or reinforcer is delivered consistently. But what happens when desired outcomes do not occur consistently, such as when an infant's cues regarding their needs are responded to inconsistently or not at all? Such is the experience of infants where there are gross deficiencies in CARE and for those who have an attachment disorder. To understand these children better, I will focus on the results of follow-up experiments conducted by Skinner with respect to the animals that received a food reward inconsistently or not at all.

After he had conditioned certain animals to expect a food reward on an inconsistent basis for presses of the lever in the Skinner Box, Skinner changed the conditions under which food was delivered. He further tested the responses of this group of animals to two new conditions. In the first condition he switched the animals from an inconsistent reinforcement regime to a consistent reinforcement regime. In the second condition he switched the animals from an inconsistent reinforcement regime to a no reinforcement regime. That is, food was either delivered consistently or not at all.

This is where it gets really interesting for our understanding of children who have an attachment disorder. Both of these new groups were slow to learn that conditions had changed. Both groups continued to press the lever at a high rate and with great persistence. The animals who now received a pellet of food for every press of the lever ended up with a pile of uneaten food at the mouth of the chute. The animals that no longer received food continued to press the lever for a long time after food was no longer delivered.

In contrast, the animals that originally had not received food for presses of the lever continued to be uninterested in the lever, even after they were switched to a condition where a food reward was on offer.

These findings are of particular relevance to children who have an attachment disorder. What we can conclude from these results is that the children have learnt one or other of two things:

- that they have to perform an action or actions that previously resulted in a need being satisfied (albeit, inconsistently) with a high rate and great persistence in order to be reassured that needs provision will occur

- that they cannot rely on others for the satisfaction of their needs.

If this was not problematic enough, if you remove the child from an inconsistently responsive or unresponsive environment and put them in a consistently responsive one, such as occurs when a child is placed in long-term foster, adoptive or kinship care, they continue to behave as if they are in the original care environment. They continue to be inordinately preoccupied with their needs and prone to attempting compulsively to satisfy their needs through persistent demanding behaviour or deceptive, self-reliant means.

Take food, for example. Children who have an attachment disorder are often preoccupied with accessibility to food, make frequent requests for food even when full, will gorge themselves until they are sick if allowed unrestricted access to large amounts of food, will steal food and will hide and hoard food. All of this occurs regardless of the whether they are hungry or not and whether they receive adequate food or not. For these children, their obsession with food is likely to reflect their enduring concern regarding accessibility to this most basic need and the sensitive responsiveness of others to this need.

A further consequence of inconsistent and inadequate needs provision is that many children who have an attachment disorder fail to develop a clear idea of how to access needs provision consistently and successfully in a socially accepted way (e.g. asking). Rather, they present their caregivers with a diverse range of behaviours and affective displays in the hope that one might elicit needs provision, or secure access to needs provision via manipulation or deceit. The failure to develop and demonstrate consistent, successful and socially sanctioned strategies to access needs provision is most obvious among children whose early attachments might be classified as *disorganised*. Disorganised attachment behaviour becomes self-reinforcing, as adults fail to understand, feel overwhelmed by and institute behavioural sanctions in response to behaviour that is perceived by them as aberrant and/or age-inappropriate, notwithstanding the fact that it is the child's own manner of signalling that they require a response to a need.

The enduring belief held by children who have an attachment disorder that adult caregivers are unreliable or unresponsive with regard to needs provision compounds the anxiety and heightened arousal of children who have already experienced grossly deficient CARE. As a result, they remain prone to aberrant behaviour associated with activation of the fight-flight-freeze response. This generally results in conflict with others, which reinforces the child's perception of the world and others as harsh and uncaring, and of themselves as bad, undeserving and powerless. The outcome is a self-reinforcing cycle of maladjustment, as reflected in Figure 2.6.

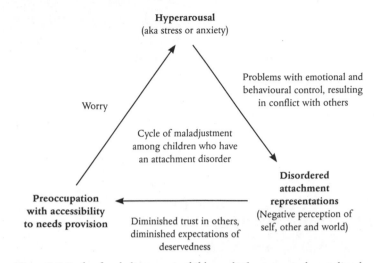

Figure 2.6 Cycle of maladjustment in children who have an attachment disorder

SPECIFIC MANIFESTATIONS OF DEFICITS IN CARE

In conjunction with the broader consequences for attachment, arousal and learning, gross deficiencies in CARE manifest in identifiable ways among children who have an attachment disorder. As a result of the absence of *consistency* in their first care environment(s), children who have an attachment disorder present as being anxious about, and preoccupied with, controlling and regulating their environment through alternately charming and hostile/distancing behaviour in order to promote a sense of a predictable world and associated feelings of safety. The consequence of gross deficiencies in *accessibility* to a caregiving adult result in either indiscriminate sociability or restricted social interest, and reduced dependency on adults in a caregiving role. Gross deficiencies in *responsiveness* of the infant's first caretakers manifest in poor self-concept, poor self-care, bodily function disturbances (e.g. wetting and soiling – these can also be a consequence of chronic hyperarousal and impaired muscle control), low expectations of deservedness and limited disclosure of inner world and poor inner-state language. Finally, gross deficiencies in *emotional connectedness* to a caring adult result in restricted range of affect, inconsistent affect, reduced empathy, reduced shared emotional experience and reduced attempts to regulate emotions and behaviour out of concern for how it impacts on other people (known as co-regulation).

WHAT DOES ATTACHMENT DISORDER LOOK LIKE?

Many children who have an attachment disorder show both an avoidance of intimacy and extreme attempts to control close relationships coercively using threatening, angry or menacing behaviours and/or seductive, charming or demanding behaviours. As close relationships for these children have often led to abuse, fear and hurt (shame and rejection), closeness becomes equated with distress or danger and intimacy becomes something to be resisted. The closer a caregiver tries to get to the child or the more love they show, the more threatening they become to the child. Nevertheless, the child who has an attachment disorder is also uncomfortable with too much distance from the caregiver and associated concern that the caregiver may no longer be under their direct influence. A vicious cycle often ensues, whereby the child draws the caregiver closer through demanding or charming behaviours, only to distance them when they come too close, and then draw the caregiver back in when the distance (physical and/or emotional) becomes too great again. The child's behaviour serves to demand attention and a caregiver response to their needs, punish and distance the caregiver, and release pent-up frustration and anger.[53]

Other children who have an attachment disorder exhibit diffuse attachments, as manifested by indiscriminate sociability and a marked inability to exhibit appropriate selective attachments. Such children are typically perceived to be charming and gregarious, are likely to be excessively friendly towards strangers and do not display appropriate selectivity and orientation towards attachment figures when attachment behaviours are activated (e.g. when hurt, unwell, frightened, hungry).

Where care arrangements change (e.g. children in foster or adoptive care), children who have an attachment disorder often compulsively re-enact their maladaptive interactions with their new caregivers. Like other children, they feel safe and reassured in association with people behaving in predictable and expected ways. As they expect caregivers to be angry and threatening, or undependable and rejecting, they often behave in a manner that precipitates similar behaviour in their new caregivers, thus confirming their belief systems, which is reassuring, and perpetuating the cycle. Their belief systems also tell them that caregivers cannot be trusted or relied upon to understand them and meet their needs. Children who have an attachment disorder conclude that they are the only person they can depend upon and the only way to get their needs met is to take matters into their own hands. The outcome is the exhibition of controlling, manipulative behaviours and/or deceptive and deceitful behaviours arising from a preoccupation with accessibility to needs provision.

The controlling and manipulative behaviours of children who have an attachment disorder typically take the form of angry, aggressive and destructive behaviours, charming and seductive behaviours or a combination of these. From the first days of life, the infant uses affective displays, such as crying and smiling, to command the attention of their caregivers. Throughout childhood, children who have an attachment disorder continue to rely on affective displays to assure attention to their needs, punish and distance their caregivers and release pent-up anxiety/arousal.

Children who have an attachment disorder seek to communicate their thoughts, feelings and needs through their behaviour and affective displays, much like a preverbal child. In addition to smiling and crying, behaviours and affective displays used to communicate thoughts, feelings and needs might include sulking, tantrums, aggression, destructiveness, clinginess and repetitive actions to secure attention (e.g. turning the TV off, turning lights on and off). As a result of neglectful care and associated mistrust of others, they often do not progress to the stage of articulating their thoughts, feelings, wishes and needs when they acquire the language to do so. They consider controlling, manipulative behaviours and affective displays to be a more effective strategy. When caregivers ignore, admonish or discipline aberrant behaviour and affective displays, the child who has an attachment disorder feels misunderstood and their belief that their caregivers are uncaring and unresponsive is again confirmed. They see punishment as arbitrary, cruel and rejecting. Their behaviour reflects their expectation of caregiver unavailability, rejection and/or maltreatment, and the imposition of punishment serves to confirm these expectations.[54]

When caregivers learn that love and patience is not enough for these children, they can feel discouraged and reject the child, further contributing to the child's self-concept of being unlovable and their caregivers as rejecting. Caregivers may even develop negative and abusive feelings towards the child. Because these children can be superficially charming to others, especially to those who do not present the threat of intimacy, professionals may see the caregivers as unduly harsh or rejecting.

Children who have an attachment disorder demonstrate an apparent lack of concern for maintaining close and loving relationships with their adult caregivers. As a result, compared with other children they are relatively unconcerned about the impact of their behaviour on their relationship with others. Rather, they develop a range of aberrant behaviours that assure accessibility to needs provision while also punishing and distancing their caregivers. In turn, the caregivers can experience feelings of revulsion and loathing towards the child that impact negatively upon their care of the child and further reinforce the child's negative attributions or beliefs about the relationship. The result, in many cases, where carers lack knowledge and understanding of attachment disorder, is the breakdown of the child's care arrangements, sometimes occurring continually. Unfortunately, this often only serves to reinforce the child's negative attachment representations.

So now we have built up a picture of what a child who has an attachment disorder looks like, thereby extending the descriptions offered in the DSM-5 and assisting in their detection, diagnosis and treatment. For ease of reference I have summarised these in Table 2.1. Children who have an attachment disorder exhibit some or all of the characteristics presented in Table 2.1 more frequently and with greater intensity and duration than one might normally expect from same-aged children (more on this below).

Table 2.1 Signs and symptoms of an attachment disorder in children

DSM-5 criteria	Manifestations	
RAD	Reduced dependency and responsiveness to care Disturbed emotions and emotional responsiveness to others	
DSED	Reduced dependency Overfamiliarity Indiscriminate sociability	

Gross deficiencies in CARE	Manifestations	
Maladaptive perception of self	Poor self-concept Poor self-care	Bodily function disturbances (e.g. wetting, soiling) Low expectations of deservedness
Maladaptive perception of other	Avoidance of engagement/ intimacy Lack of empathy	Habitual mistrust Superficial charm
Maladaptive perception of the social world	Preoccupation with: • safety • fairness	• rules • consistency • knowing
Hyperarousal (anxiety)	Aggression Hyperactivity Destructiveness Inattention Avoidance	Dissociation Emotional lability (instability) Learning problems/ delays Watchfulness/ hypervigilance Low resilience
Preoccupation with accessibility to needs provision	Controlling Demanding Manipulative	Charming Deceitful

Deficiencies in consistency	Controlling Demanding Manipulative Charming/seductive	To relieve habitual feelings of uncertainty and promote feelings of interpersonal safety and access to needs provision
Deficiencies in accessibility	Indiscriminate sociability or restricted social interest Reduced dependency	Arising from a poor understanding of what a caregiver represents
Deficiencies in responsiveness	Poor self-concept Poor self-care Bodily function disturbances (e.g. wetting, soiling)	Low expectations of deservedness Limited disclosure of inner world and associated poor inner-state language
Deficiencies in emotional connectedness	Restricted range of affect Inconsistent affect Reduced empathy	Reduced shared emotional experience Reduced co-regulation

WHEN SHOULD A DIAGNOSIS OF ATTACHMENT DISORDER BE CONSIDERED?

So, when might you consider a diagnosis of RAD or DSED? The simple answer is, when a child with whom you are involved exhibits social, emotional and behavioural disturbance in the context of their interactions and relationships with others, where the child has a known history of grossly deficient CARE and where the child's history of grossly deficient CARE is the best explanation for their disturbed presentation. That is, it is not only what they do, but also why they do it that is an important consideration in diagnosis. This is what differentiates attachment disorders from, say, Autism Spectrum Disorder, where the disturbances arise from biological as opposed to

CARE factors. This is referred to as differential diagnosis and is a vital component of any diagnostic process.

Another consideration to bear in mind is that not all children who display social, emotional and/or behavioural difficulties or disturbances warrant a clinical diagnosis. In fact, most problematic behaviours and affective displays (including the ones in Table 2.1) are exhibited by all children at least some of the time. That is, normality and abnormality generally are not determined by the presence or absence of social, emotional and behavioural disturbance. Rather, normality and abnormality are differentiated by frequency, intensity and duration of the social, emotional and behavioural disturbance. As to what the social, emotional and behavioural disturbances that children who have an attachment disorder present with, I have endeavoured to describe typical aspects of their presentation in this chapter.

Your decision-making process starts with observing the child. Does the child's disturbance in social, emotional and behavioural functioning occur in more than one setting? If the child's maladjustment is limited to one setting, then it is likely that there is some aspect of the setting that is responsible for the child's maladjustment and not necessarily a disorder such as RAD or DSED. In order for a diagnosis of RAD or DSED to be made, the child must show maladjustment in most, if not all, environments.

The next step in your decision-making is to determine whether the child's maladjustment occurs frequently, intensively and for an extended duration. Maladjustment that occurs intermittently is unlikely to be consistent with RAD or DSED.

The third aspect of your decision-making is to identify whether the child's maladjustment is the likely result of gross deficiencies in CARE during infancy and early childhood. If so, and if the above two steps are satisfied in favour of further consideration of an attachment disorder, only then would you consider making (in the case of suitably qualified and experienced psychiatrists, psychologists and other mental health professionals) or seeking professional investigation of (in the case of a caregiver or other professional involved with the child, e.g. a teacher) a diagnosis of RAD or DSED.

CHAPTER SUMMARY

- Over the last three decades, the term 'attachment disorder' has entered into common usage among professionals and carers who interact with children who display markedly disturbed and developmentally inappropriate relatedness to others.

- In the fifth and latest edition of the Diagnostic and Statistical Manual of Mental Disorders (DSM-5) two diagnoses are relevant to the discussion of what an attachment disorder is, what it looks like and when the diagnosis should be used – Reactive Attachment Disorder (RAD) and Disinhibited Social Engagement Disorder (DSED).

- RAD might be considered when children show limited dependency on others for comfort, support, protection and nurturance, and limited response to comfort from an adult in a caregiving role. Children with RAD must also show disturbances of emotion and emotional responsiveness to others.

- DSED might be considered when a child displays culturally inappropriate, overly familiar behaviour with relative strangers. They may display reduced or absence reticence to engage or even go off with unfamiliar adults, overly familiar verbal and physical behaviours and diminished or absent checking back with an adult caregiver, including in unfamiliar situations.

- There is a common feature to both disorders – the condition is understood to have arisen as a result of grossly deficient care, as evidenced by either the persistent absence of a caregiver response to the infant's basic needs for comfort, stimulation and affection or where there is not the opportunity for the development of stable, selective attachments; such as occurs in rotational care environments and institutional care, or where there are repeated changes in foster care placement.

- CARE influences the type of attachment, or attachment style, a child develops. The way a child relates to themselves, others and their world is, in turn, impacted by attachment formation and attachment style. As a result of their attachment experiences, and through relating to their primary attachment figures, children develop a sense of themselves, who and what others represent and what relating to them is like and what interacting with the world is like. This sense of themselves, others and the world is represented in a set of interrelated beliefs that are commonly referred to as attachment representations or internal working models.[55, 56, 57, 58, 59]

- The attachment representations of children who have an attachment disorder are primarily negative, leaving them prone to disturbed relatedness with others, their world and even their own self.

- A consequence of the persistent and inconsistently relieved distress arising under conditions of neglectful (and abusive) CARE is persistently elevated *arousal*, leaving children who have an attachment disorder chronically under the influence of the inner structures of their brain and the functions they serve.

- A further consequence of gross deficiencies in CARE is that many children who have an attachment disorder are intensely preoccupied with historically inconsistently met or unmet needs and fail to develop a clear idea of how to consistently and successfully access needs provision in a socially accepted way (e.g. asking).

- A diagnosis of RAD or DSED might be considered when a child with whom you are involved exhibits social, emotional and behavioural disturbance in the context of their interactions and relationships with others, where the child has a known history of grossly deficient CARE and where the child's history of grossly deficient CARE is the best explanation for their disturbed presentation.

MATTHEW'S STORY CONTINUED

Matthew was referred to a psychologist when he was six years old. By that time he was being repeatedly suspended from school and his latest foster placement was at breaking point. In his initial interview with the psychologist, Matthew was friendly but watchful. He was compliant when directed but resistant when asked. He was scruffy and smelled of urine and of having soiled. On a number of occasions during the interview he asked where his foster carer was and sought to check on her whereabouts. He expressed an ambivalent perception of school. He identified it as a place where games were played but lamented the fact that there were so many rules. He complained that his teacher shouted too much and that his peers bullied him. He grandiosely claimed that he was good at 'everything' and not so good at 'nothing'.

He asserted that he made himself happy and no one made him angry, sad or scared, or hurt him or hurt his feelings. He confidently claimed that he looked after himself when he was unwell, that he 'let it bleed' when he was hurt and that he wanted 'nobody' to cuddle him when sad or protect him when scared.

At her own interview Matthew's foster carer, his fifth, reported that that Matthew demanded her attention and followed her around constantly, even to the toilet. She complained that his stomach was a 'bottomless pit' and that stealing food was a problem at home and school. She reported that he was a poor sleeper, often laying awake until midnight and appearing to go 'ten rounds with Mike Tyson' while he slept. She suspected that he roamed the house, taking food and other items, while she slept. She considered that he used anger as a tool to intimidate and manipulate people, and she recalled incidents where his angry outbursts became so intense and so prolonged that he appeared zoned out and no longer connected with his surroundings. She added that extreme tantrums could be precipitated by the slightest provocation, such as asking him to put his shoes in his room. She acknowledged that he did not like being told what to do and preferred to be the boss. She perceived that despite his bravado he was a frightened little boy at heart, being reluctant to leave the home and having a tendency to give up easily when confronted with new experiences. She considered that this was behind many of his problems at school, which included oppositional and defiant behaviours towards teaching staff and controlling and aggressive behaviours towards his peers. She claimed that caring for Matthew was like being on an emotional rollercoaster, and she acknowledged feeling harassed and defeated.

More generally, Matthew's foster carer reported that Matthew received speech therapy for immature articulation of sounds in words. She understood that the delays in his speech stemmed from a suspected history of recurrent ear infections. She recalled that his suspected history of ear infections and associated hearing problems were only realised in association with investigations into his immature speech some months after he entered her care as a three-year-old. She confirmed that Matthew had entered her care in association with his previous placement breaking down due to his foster carer having reported to child-protection authorities that she was unable to cope with Matthew's increasingly demanding behaviour and tantrums.

CHAPTER **3**

CARE TO PROMOTE ATTACHMENT SECURITY

In this chapter I want to introduce you to a set of practical ideas and strategies concerning the care of children who have an attachment disorder, which promote attachment security, optimal arousal and new learning that needs are understood and important and will be responded to reliably and consistently through conventional care. I am hoping that you will see that they are common sense and that you might respond with 'I already do that'. There are few things worse in the care and management of children who have an attachment disorder than attempting to implement a raft of changes to the way in which you care for and manage them, only to doubt the utility of these changes as the child reacts badly to change (remember, inconsistency is stressful) and subsequently abandon them. It is one of the great ironies of caring for children who have an attachment disorder that the more we try (and subsequently abandon) the latest recommended strategy or strategies for addressing some aspect of the maladjustment of these children, the more we inadvertently replicate one of the deficient aspects of the care environment in which the attachment disorder originally arose – *inconsistency*. Rather, it is my preference to discuss ideas that you most likely already have and care and management strategies that you already implement, as this allows for the greatest consistency in ongoing therapeutic care. I am hoping that it also makes you feel as though you are not a complete failure and that you are already doing many things right! I simply recommend that you selectively prioritise aspects of conventional care and management that promote attachment security and enrich the child's experience of them.

I do hope that you will read on and not put the book down, citing the fact that I have just said that you already do the things that are helpful in promoting attachment security. It is one of the risks of recommending straightforward strategies for complex problems. People tend to doubt them, but I have also found that people do not consistently implement complex strategies over time and in the face of the day-to-day challenges of caring for a child who has an attachment disorder. I would also advise you here that the approach I recommend in this chapter forms part of the Triple-A Model of Therapeutic Care. Triple-A is implemented through my own practice in South Australia and in an organised way with foster carers in Donegal, Ireland. Early results from the programme attest to its relevance to the care of children who are fostered and its effectiveness in promoting improved adjustment in children.[60]

Finally, I also want to make the point that this chapter is relevant to all adults in a caregiving role who engage with children who have an attachment disorder. This includes parents, foster parents, adoptive parents, kinship carers (e.g. aunts, uncles, grandparents) and youth workers. It is also relevant to the care and management of children who have an attachment disorder in the classroom, and so is relevant to teachers and other staff in schools. It is relevant to mental health professionals who treat these children and support adults who care for them. Moreover, it is relevant to the care of all children where the goal is the promotion of attachment security.

THE IMPORTANCE OF PROMOTING STRONG AND SECURE ATTACHMENT RELATIONSHIPS

Before I get into the ideas and care and management behaviours that promote attachment security and recovery from an attachment disorder, I just want to remind readers of a couple of reasons why we undertake this endeavour.

The first reason is that children who have an attachment disorder are not happy. At times they may look happy, such as when they smile when your coping resources are overwhelmed and you say or do something you regret. But this is not the circumstance under which we want them to experience happiness, and most of the time they are anxious and preoccupied anyway. Rather, I would contend that we would like them to feel happy about being a good, capable and deserving person who enjoys deep, lasting and meaningful connections with others, including with their life partner and with their own children. That is, our endeavours to promote attachment security among children who have an attachment disorder promotes a happy, healthy life and, potentially, breaks the cycle of intergenerational transmission of abuse, neglect and attachment disorder.

A second reason is that children who are raised in stable and loving homes where they develop a secure attachment style grow to respect and value the relationship they have with others. Out of respect for their own worth and deservedness, the rights of others and the relationships they maintain with significant people in their lives, they learn from their transgressions and increasingly conform to conventions regarding what is acceptable behaviour out of a concern for maintaining close and loving relationships with significant others.

Unfortunately, having been denied the experience of meaningful connection with adults in a caregiving role who promote a strong and healthy sense of their worth, competency and deservedness and the value of being and remaining on good terms with others, the behaviour of children who have an attachment disorder is not as strongly regulated by concern for the relationships they have with others. Rather, they perceive relationships as something to be avoided or people as a means to an end. That end is feelings of interpersonal safety and wellbeing arising from a feeling of being able to control the behaviour of others in order to satisfy themselves that their needs will be met. They may not have a relationship with anyone in their life that they respect and value sufficiently for the relationship to be a powerful regulating influence over their behaviour. They are prone to unregulated, antisocial behaviour and affective displays, for which they experience little guilt or remorse.

Figure 3.1 illustrates the relationship between attachment, social integration and behaviour. Essentially, secure attachment representations predispose a child/person to making and maintaining quality relationships with family, friends and others in their social world. Secure individuals are integrated into a social network and largely conform to the moral and ethical values and standards of behaviour of their network. Their network tends to hold values that are consistent with broader moral and ethical values and conventional standards of behaviour in society, as secure individuals are, by definition, well-adjusted. In contrast, children with attachment disorder end up being less integrated into mainstream society. As a result, they are less likely to conform to conventional standards of behaviour. Though they may form their own social networks, these are most likely to comprise similarly maladjusted individuals whose moral and ethical values and standards of behaviour reflect baser needs (e.g. violent criminal gangs). They are more likely to commit antisocial and unconscionable acts in the pursuit of securing needs provision. It follows that the resolution of attachment problems is likely to benefit the whole community as well as the individual.

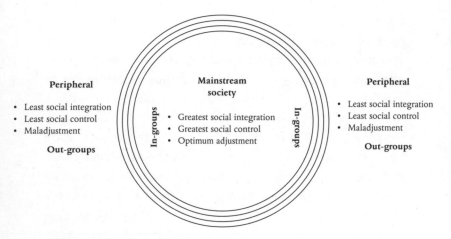

Figure 3.1 *The relationship between social integration, social control and adjustment*

In sum, the remediation of attachment disorders promotes individual happiness and the welfare and wellbeing of the community as a whole.

BACK TO BASICS – THE CARE MODEL

In Chapter 1, I introduced four dimensions of *care* that are directly implicated in attachment security and attachment style. Using the simple acronym CARE, I showed how variations along each dimension are implicated in attachment security, insecurity and disorganisation. I proposed that attachment security arises under conditions of *consistency* in the care environment, including the consistent presence of an *accessible, responsive* and *emotionally connected* attachment figure. In Chapter 2, I showed how grossly deficient CARE plays a direct role in the aetiology of attachment disorders and the presentation of children with these conditions, including a disordered belief about self, other and world, hyperarousal and anxiety proneness, and their preoccupation with accessibility to needs provision. In any endeavour to promote attachment security and recovery from an attachment disorder we must offer new *experiences* of CARE, thereby promoting new learning, including remedial learning about the consistency, accessibility, responsiveness and emotional connectedness of caregiving adults that facilitates happiness and adherence to behavioural conventions.

You may note that I referred to 'new *experiences* of CARE'. I am being very deliberate in my choice of words here. Just as the human infant has learnt about consistency, accessibility, responsiveness and emotional connectedness of adults in a caregiving role via experience, so will children who have an attachment disorder achieve new learning via new experiences that challenge their old learning. Certainly, they will not learn by being told that they have got it all wrong, that we are there for them, that we understand them and that we feel emotionally connected to them. Not only will they doubt the sincerity of our words, they may also treat them as an invitation to challenge them. They will think that we are being dishonest and, therefore, untrustworthy. They are likely to feel less understood than ever, as our words would be inconsistent with their entrenched, unhelpful beliefs about themselves, others and their world.

Rather, we need to offer experiences of enriched CARE. Enriched CARE, particularly where it confines itself to conventional care and management behaviours, represents the best hope of subtly challenging and sneaking through the carefully tended defences of the child who has an attachment disorder. Through enriched CARE we stand the best chance of promoting attachment security, reducing arousal and associated anxiety proneness, and facilitating new learning that their needs are understood and important and will be responded to through conventional care and without them having to go to great lengths to make it so.

Consistency

In Chapter 1, I wrote about how the optimal conditions for learning what one needs to do to survive and thrive in the world is when an action is consistently followed by a desired outcome. What the human infant learns about how dependable their attachment figure(s) is for satisfaction of their needs is dependent on how consistently they receive a satisfying caregiving response to their cues. In an inconsistent or unresponsive care environment, the infant's learning is impaired. This is the experience of children who have an attachment disorder. The result is a pervasive belief that the world is an unpredictable and uncaring place. This sense of the unpredictability of the world is anxiety evoking, compounding the hyperarousal of the child who has an attachment disorder and exacerbating their proneness to behaviours associated with the fight-flight-freeze response and the cycle of maladjustment represented in Figure 2.6 on page 57.

Consistency is the essential precondition for success in all of our endeavours to assist children who have an attachment disorder. Whatever we do, we must do it consistently. As mentioned earlier, it is counter-productive to make substantial changes to the way in which you care for and manage a child, only to revert to old patterns of caregiving and relating, or try something else, when it gets too hard or you feel overwhelmed by the challenges arising from the child's own reactivity to change.

Rather, only do what you can manage to do consistently. Only do what you can keep doing over time. This applies to all of the caregiving and relating behaviours and strategies that I will present across the balance of this chapter. Set routines and caregiving rituals that are part of your existing behavioural repertoire and easy to maintain. In doing so you will avoid falling into the trap of re-enacting aspects of the care environment that were responsible for the development of the attachment disorder in the first place.

For example, if you plan to implement a bedtime ritual, only do so if you can do it every night. Similarly, if you plan to engage in special time with the child, do not allocate an hour per day for the first three days, only to find that on the fourth and fifth day you run out of time and the child's behaviour does not warrant special time anyway. This is confusing and upsetting for the child who has an attachment disorder. It is experienced by them as only being worthy of your attention when all other priorities are attended to and only if they are good, which they struggle to see themselves as being. I will return to this issue consistently as I present further aspects of therapeutic caregiving and management across the balance of this chapter.

Consistency is important in behaviour management as well. Children who have an attachment disorder require behaviour management, though delivered in isolation it is rarely effective and often has the effect of compounding the maladjustment of these children. Children who have an attachment disorder are prone to communicating about their needs and experiences via their behaviour. This is another consequence of gross deficiencies in CARE, whereby the child who has an attachment disorder has not had the opportunity to learn the words that adequately describe their experience and to express themselves. In addition, their motivation to communicate verbally is low, as they anticipate disinterest and disregard for their needs. They are also preoccupied with their needs and show a high rate of, and great persistence in, behaviour whose purpose is to satisfy needs that were met inconsistently or not at all. Viewed in this way, the child who has an attachment disorder sees their behaviour as justified and a justifiable response to what they perceive to be a harsh world. Behaviour management is experienced as arbitrary and cruel and further evidence that that their needs and intentions do not matter, thereby compounding maladaptive attachment representations.

In a later section I will present further information about how to implement behaviour management in a way that reduces the risk of reinforcing the maladaptive attachment representations, hyperarousal and preoccupation with accessibility to needs provision of the child who has an attachment disorder. For now, I will also make the point that the most common methods of behaviour management, including removing the desired outcome of an unwanted behaviour through ignoring, response prevention and time out, or through punishing unwanted behaviour, are generally ineffective at stopping the unwanted behaviour and compound the maladjustment of the child who has an attachment disorder. This is because you have to remove the desired outcome every time the child engages in the unwanted behaviour for the behaviour to eventually be extinguished. If you cannot prevent the desired outcome each and every time the child engages in the unwanted behaviour, the behaviour is being *inconsistently* reinforced. What you now know about this is that behaviours, including unwanted ones, appear with high rate and great persistence when they are inconsistently reinforced. So if you cannot consistently remove or prevent the desired outcome of the behaviour, you will see more of it. In the case of punishment of unwanted behaviour, this only heightens the distress of the child who has an attachment disorder, increasingly their propensity to engage in behaviours associated with the fight-flight-freeze response and compounding their maladjustment.

So, the take-home message here is: consistency is important in everything you undertake to do to promote attachment security and recovery from attachment disorder.

Accessibility

In September 2014 Secure Start® conducted an online survey of carers of 'looked-after children' (defined as children who do not live with a birth parent(s) and are in a relative or kinship care placement, adoptive placement, foster placement or residential care placement), in which responses were received from 157 carers over a one-week period. Respondents to the survey were provided with a list of behaviours commonly observed among children in out-of-home care and with a history of early or developmental trauma (aka abuse and neglect), as represented in Table 3.1, and asked to indicate which behaviours they saw in the children in their care that were causing them concern. They were asked to identify as many behaviours from the list as they wished. Consider the behaviours in the table below and see if you can guess what was the most reported behaviour of concern. The answer may surprise you.

Table 3.1 Behaviours seen in children in out-of-home care

Characteristic	Manifestations
Maladaptive perception of self	Poor self-concept Poor self-care Bodily function disturbances (e.g. wetting, soiling) Low expectations of deservedness
Maladaptive perception of other	Avoidance of engagement/intimacy Lack of empathy Habitual mistrust Superficial charm
Maladaptive perception of the social world	Preoccupation with safety Preoccupation with fairness Preoccupation with rules Preoccupation with consistency Preoccupation with knowing
Hyperarousal (anxiety)	Aggression Hyperactivity Destructiveness Inattention Dissociation Emotional lability (Instability) Developmental/learning problems/delays Watchfulness/hypervigilance
Preoccupation with accessibility to needs provision	Controlling Demanding Manipulative Charming Deceitful

The most commonly reported behaviour among the respondent carers was that the children were *demanding*. Carers of children who have experienced gross deficiencies in CARE during infancy often report they:

- can't speak to visitors without the child compulsively (and seemingly needlessly) intruding and interrupting

- can't take phone calls while the child is present

- can't even go to the toilet or have a shower without the child coercively seeking to maintain the carer's attention on them.

They also report that these children:

- are preoccupied with them
- show an apparent fear that they will be forgotten
- show an apparent fear that they will be abandoned
- show an apparent fear that their carers will not respond to them when truly needed…

…if their carers are not attending to them *all the time.*

These are irrational fears that stem from their experience of adults in a caregiving role having been inconsistently accessible during infancy.

So, how do you assure the child who has an attachment disorder that adults in a caregiving role are available and willing to attend to the child and, further, that the child is worthy and deserving of CARE, including the children who have effectively given up on adults being accessible to them and have decided that they can only rely on themselves? Well, you have two options. The first option is you can be there for the child every single time they need you. How will that help if the child exhibits reduced dependency and rarely shows that they need you? How long can that last, notwithstanding your best intentions, for the inordinately demanding child? Remember, if you cannot be there for them every time they need you, you have created an inconsistent reinforcement situation that runs the risk of perpetuating and amplifying the child's preoccupation with your accessibility and behaviours to demand your proximity to them.

Think of the animals in the Skinner experiments. How would you assure them of access to food and stop them pressing the lever with a high rate and great persistence? The answer is that you put the food in the cage. You attend to the need proactively. In the case of the child who has an attachment disorder, you attend to them before they do anything to secure your attention.

Think of all the times you have the thought that things are quiet and you must go and check on a child. This is what I am talking about. You already do it. Think about the difference between the friend you only ever speak to when you call them or the friend who calls you. Which one do you consider to be the more reliable friend? I am guessing it is the one who rings you.

My recommendation is that you initiate brief interactions with the child at least one additional time per day. Only set out to do what you can do consistently and maintain over time. I recommend that you do it regularly and consistently. I want you to enrich the child's experience of you doing it. You need to get in first, before they do anything to secure your attention. If you primarily orient to them when they do something to secure your proximity, they think you are only doing it because they made you. If you orient to them proactively, they will experience that you are accessible and interested in them and their being worthy and deserving of the same.

Responsiveness

Responsiveness involves assuring children that their thoughts, feelings, intentions and needs are understood and important, and that they will be responded to reliably and consistently as part of conventional caregiving. Responsiveness is crucial for the promotion of strong and enduring beliefs about the sensitivity of adults in a caregiving role and the worth and deservedness of the child. Children who experienced gross deficiencies in CARE have low expectations of the sensitivity and responsiveness of adults in a caregiving role and low expectations regarding their own deservedness of a caregiving response. Enriching the child who has an attachment disorder's experience of the responsiveness of adults in a caregiving role is crucial to promoting strong and healthy attachment representations, optimal arousal and reduced anxiety about accessibility to needs provision.

Enriching responsiveness requires that caregivers do three things – hold appropriate developmental expectations, communicate understanding of the child's thoughts, feelings, intentions and needs and address those needs proactively.

Holding appropriate developmental expectations

The fundamental goal of parenting children who have an attachment disorder should be to assist them to increasingly adopt and live by more secure attachment representations of themselves, others and their world. In achieving this goal, it is important to view the behaviour of children who have an attachment disorder as developmentally appropriate, if not age-appropriate. Development unfolds in a sequence of steps built on previous successes and achievements, and these children have experienced inconsistent needs provision, major disruptions and losses that have been disruptive of their social and emotional development. In effect, they have social and emotional needs that are akin to those of a very young child. Their attempts to get their needs met is reflected in behavioural strategies and affective displays that are also typically used by very young children to draw attention to their needs and derive feelings of safety and security. These children generally do not verbalise their needs, fail to regulate their negative affect and engage in aberrant behaviour and affective displays to draw attention to their needs, secure a caregiver response and ventilate pent-up anxiety/hyperarousal. Like other children, they require caregiver involvement and love, nurturance, guidance, acknowledgement and acceptance of a range of affect and soothing when they are distressed. However, unlike other children, their caregivers may fail to respond to these needs as they become preoccupied with managing what they perceive to be age-inappropriate, aberrant behaviour and affective displays that are the child's main strategy for expressing their needs and feelings.

In contrast to the normal adult response when a baby cries loudly because it is hungry, it is a common occurrence by the time a child reaches school age for adults to expect a child to express their needs (e.g. hunger) verbally and to admonish the child for behaviours that are considered to be inappropriate to context (e.g. crying for food), even if they are the child's way of expressing a need, in order to facilitate their learning regarding acceptable behaviour and needs expression and conformity to societal expectations regarding these (Figure 3.2). This is a problem for children who have an attachment disorder, who express their needs primarily through behaviour. Children who have an attachment disorder require *a response to the need as well as the behaviour* that serves to draw attention to the need in the same way that one responds to the behavioural expressions of a preverbal child (Figure 3.3). Without this, the child will continue to be unsure about the sensitivity and responsiveness of others to their needs, their perception of the reliability and trustworthiness of others will remain disturbed, and their capacity to empathise with others will be limited. The consequences of these include ongoing unregulated behaviour and affect, antisocial behaviour and a lifetime of impairment in their wellbeing and adjustment.

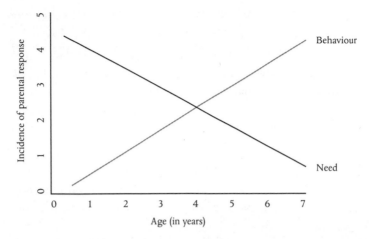

Figure 3.2 Normal patterns of caregiver response to behavioural expressions of needs in children

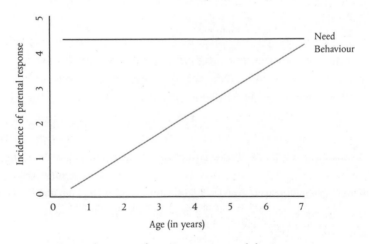

Figure 3.3 Required patterns of caregiver response to behaviour and needs for children who have an attachment disorder

Communicating understanding

Children who experienced gross deficiencies in their early CARE and have an attachment disorder are typically unable and/or unwilling to express their thoughts, feelings, intentions and needs verbally. Their development has been compromised through the absence of a consistently accessible, responsive and emotionally connected adult caregiver. When they do express themselves it is often in behaviour and affective displays that are poorly understood for what they represent. Of further concern is that the intent behind the behaviour or affective display goes unacknowledged and, rather, is responded to with cajoling, admonition, ignoring or discipline. This leaves the child who has an attachment disorder feeling unheard and misunderstood, and their thoughts, feelings, intentions and needs are un-responded to, thereby compounding their distress, their preoccupations with their needs and their negativistic attachment representations.

You cannot simply tell a child who has an attachment disorder that their thoughts, feelings, intentions and needs are understood and important and will be responded to. Rather, they need to experience this, just as the infant does when they get fed when they are hungry, burped when they have tummy pain, changed when they are dirty and cuddled when they require soothing, all without having words to express themselves.

In order to enrich the experience of the child who has an attachment disorder that their thoughts, feelings, intentions and needs are understood and important you need to consider and accept the following truism: *nobody does anything for no reason*. All behaviour is intentional and serves some function or other for the individual. Your task, in enriching the child's experience of their thoughts, feelings, intentions and needs being understood, is to observe the child and the setting and ask yourself the following question: *what is going on for the child right now?* This question should be asked and answered in your head. It is the only place for questions when attempting to communicate understanding to a child who has an attachment disorder. Asking questions of the child who has an attachment disorder offers them the experience that their thoughts, feelings, intentions and needs are *not* understood by you.

Once you have an answer to the question, you should say out loud what it is you think the child is thinking or feeling, what their intentions are/were and what need it is that they are attempting to draw attention to. Essentially, *you speak their mind.* Your answer to the question and the words you use need only be a close approximate of what is occurring in that moment for the child. You do not have to know exactly what they are thinking and feeling, why they did what they did and what need they are attempting to draw attention to and secure needs provision for. Examples of the kinds of statements you might make include the following.

- 'You like that' (e.g. when a child is playing a favourite video game or watching a favourite television show).

- 'You look like something is bothering you' (e.g. when the child trudges from the school gate with their head down).

- 'He must have done something that annoyed you' (e.g. when the child has hit another child).

- 'You hate losing' (e.g. when the child responds angrily to the vicissitudes of a board or card game).

You only need to be close. You will know when you are close, as the child will respond with relief and/or pleasure. They may orient to your face, their eyes will widen, they will let their breath out in a rush and they will say:

- 'Exactly'

- 'Finally, someone who understands'

- 'Yes!'

- 'Finally, you get it!'

They are just as likely to then disclose further detail about what is going on for them right at that moment, thus offering further opportunities to communicate interest and understanding.

Alternatively, they may show little reaction or a hostile reaction. If they show little reaction, you may be off the mark, or they may be avoiding the experience of closeness that arises when a person experiences the understanding of another. They may also respond angrily. In all of these scenarios, you have still made an impression on the child. They may initially be defensive, because the people who they previously relied on to look after them hurt them or let them down. However, you must be persistent in your efforts in communicating understanding or they will never accept healthy connection with others and never recover from their attachment disorder. It is only through sustained engagement and connection that children who have an attachment disorder will overcome their fear and associated avoidance of healthy dependency on adults in a caregiving role. So, rather than giving up on communicating understanding, I would recommend that you say:

- 'You don't like it when I think I know what you are thinking'

- 'You don't like it when I know what you are thinking'

- 'It bothers you when I understand what you are thinking…or…why you did that.'

And, then say 'I just want you to know that I am trying my best to understand you…because I care about you.' This latter statement raises a second truism that it is important to accept in the care and management of a child who has an attachment disorder: *in order to be heard you first need to listen.* Once you have communicated understanding, you have the child's attention and you are beginning to have their trust, your next words will have greater meaning or impact on the child. They are more likely to accept your statement that you care about them when you show them first that you understand them. This also applies when implementing corrective guidance following a child's misdemeanour. First, communicate understanding and then offer corrective feedback. For further explanation of this, and how to use behaviour management, I refer you to the boxed section below.

Children who have an attachment disorder often experience a deep sense of shame in association with caregiver admonishments. Unaddressed, this shame can promote ill feeling towards the caregiver and further distance the child, which, ultimately, is counter-productive in terms of achieving a close and loving caregiver–child relationship. After intervening in relation to a child's behaviour it is important to remind them that you still love them or make some other statements reflecting their positive attributes.

While the behaviour of children who have an attachment disorder is probably of the most immediate concern, it is important that the primary focus is on developing positive relationships, because without this context, no behaviour management strategies will be effective. Children who have an attachment disorder are likely to interpret discipline as arbitrary and cruel, so directions and consequences need to be delivered calmly and with empathy rather than with anger. In order to help the child deal with their feelings of shame and rage, interactive repair should be provided as soon as possible after discipline so that the child knows that they will not be rejected because of their behaviour.

Figure 3.4 illustrates how the parenting suggestions incorporated in this book can be incorporated into day-to-day behaviour management.

- In the first step, the child engages in some form of misbehaviour. Rather than verbally admonishing the child or instituting some form of punishment (e.g. time-out[61]), it is important to first take stock of the circumstances under which the behaviour occurred and verbalise understanding regarding the need, the thought and/or the feeling that gave rise to the behaviour.

- Next, a caregiver should model for the child and encourage proper expression of thoughts, feelings and needs. Then, the caregiver should explain to the child that they have choices regarding their expression of the aforementioned and the different consequences (or outcomes) that arise from each choice.

- Only after these two steps are followed should the caregiver discipline the child.

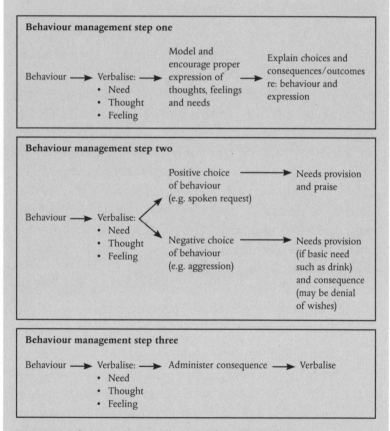

Figure 3.4 Behaviour management: putting the pieces together

When my youngest child was three years of age (i.e. newly/ incompletely verbal) he would, at times, call out 'hungry' or 'thirsty'. At other times he had a habit of standing at the refrigerator, looking to see if anyone had noticed him, stomping his foot and affecting a grumpy facial expression. If noone responded to his signal that he was hungry, thirsty or both he would angrily stomp his foot and pull off various notices held to the refrigerator with magnets and throw them to the floor. At such times I might have chosen to admonish the child verbally and require him to put the notices back on the refrigerator door. To do so would have further upset him, as he would have interpreted my response as lacking understanding and being uncaring. Rather, I would say the following: 'H, I see that you are standing at the fridge and that you are cross. I understand that you think that no one has noticed that you would like a drink.' H would sullenly acknowledge 'Yes.' I would then say: 'Well H, you need to say "Please Daddy may I have a drink?".' H would quietly and sullenly say 'Please Daddy may I have something to drink?' I would then say 'A bit louder and nicely.' He would say, more loudly and in more polite tones 'Please Daddy may I have something to drink?' I would respond with 'Of course you can. I will get it for you straight away. I will always get you a drink when you need it. All you have to do is say "Please daddy may I have something to drink?". However, if you don't ask, and stand at the fridge and stomp, I may get you a drink but I will also tell you off for making a mess of the notices on the fridge. I will even ask you to put them all back.' Although H was only three years of age, this is a vivid example of step one and can be easily applied to the older child who has an attachment disorder. Thankfully, I did not have to proceed to step two and three with H.

In the second step, the child subsequently engages in some form of behaviour, good or bad, associated with the aforementioned thought, feeling or need. On this occasion the caregiver again verbalises understanding of the thought, feeling or need. In the event that the child draws attention to the thought, feeling or need using prosocial behaviour, the caregiver responds with praise and needs provision. In the event that the child draws attention to the thought, feeling or need using antisocial behaviour, the child is admonished and a consequence may be instituted. Nevertheless, the need is acknowledged and an outcome is negotiated for needs provision. A caregiver should always respond to the need as well as the behaviour. (*I can see that you are angry and that you think no one has noticed that you would like a drink. We have already spoken about how you should use your words when you would like a drink. I will give you a drink but I would like you to help me tidy up your bedroom after I get it.*)

The final step relates to when a child has made a poor choice regarding the expression of a thought, feeling or need, and a consequence is instituted. The child may become angry and/or distressed regarding the imposition of a consequence. They need to know that there is a rationale as to why a consequence is instituted and that the caregiver understands their thoughts and feeling regarding the consequence. If this important step is missed the child who has an attachment disorder is likely to form their own pessimistic, maladaptive view regarding the intentions of the adult. Hence, the caregiver verbalises understanding and reminds the child that they have the child's best interests in mind when instituting consequences for undesirable behaviours. (*I can see that you are angry that I am making you help me tidy your room and think I am being mean. However, as your parent it is my job to love and care for you and to help you make good choices about behaviour. When I discipline you it is to help you to remember to make good choices in future.*)

In association with their excessive worry regarding adult accessibility and sensitive responsiveness, children who have an attachment disorder are often preoccupied with maintaining engagement with, and control over, the behaviour and feelings of others. This manifests in excessive clinginess, attention-seeking behaviour, demanding behaviour and overtly controlling and manipulative behaviours (e.g. superficial charm and/or bossiness). The purpose of these behaviours is to reassure the child regarding accessibility to needs provision. Unfortunately, as many such behaviours are deemed age-inappropriate or otherwise deviant, and are either ignored or punished, the child who has an attachment disorder often experiences others as mean and uncaring, with resultant feelings of anger leading to distancing behaviour, followed by coercive attempts to reconnect. In order to address this, caregivers of children who have an attachment disorder should verbalise understanding of children's accessibility concerns, provide reassurance and explain to the child how to access needs provision in a socially approved manner (e.g. asking where required, being self-reliant where appropriate).

Statements that communicate understanding of accessibility preoccupations include the following.

- 'I think that you believe that I will forget about you if we are not always together.'

- 'I think that you believe I won't notice or understand when you really need me/something.'

- 'You believe that if I don't do it [get it for you] now I will forget.'

- 'You worry that I won't come back for you.'

- 'You worry that I don't like you anymore.'

- 'You know you have done something wrong and you worry that I won't like/love you anymore.'

Communicating understanding in all the ways described above offers the child who has an attachment disorder the experience that their inner world and needs are understood and important – that they are understood and important. This is a validating experience for the child and promotes their sense of their worth and deservedness. Validation experiences act as a form of psychological vaccination against depression and other mental health concerns among teens and adults. As I like to say, *if you don't acknowledge the sadness of the sad child, how will they know that their feelings matter?*

Communicating understanding in this way also assists the child to have words to go with their experience. Having the words and the experience of being heard promotes the use of words for the expression of thoughts, feelings, intentions and needs, thereby reducing communication through aberrant behaviour and enhancing the child's opportunities to be understood and responded to with understanding by others.

Communicating understanding in this way also weakens attachment representations associated with an attachment disorder. Consider the following. It is widely accepted among mental health practitioners that the way in which a person is thinking will influence how they feel, which, in turn, will influence how they behave. How they behave will precipitate a response in others and, more often than not, the response of others is typically consistent with, and reinforcing of, the original thought. Through repetition of this cycle, the thought is strengthened and becomes a belief. I have represented this in Figure 3.5:

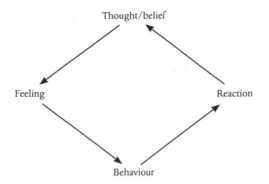

Figure 3.5 How thoughts become beliefs

Let's try an example. What happens when the child who has an attachment disorder has the following thought? *I am about to be hurt.*

More often than not the child will feel threatened/anxious/unsafe. When they feel threatened/anxious/unsafe they are prone to acting under the influence of the fight-flight-freeze response. This manifests in controlling, aggressive and destructive behaviours (fight), running and hiding (flight) and reduced responsiveness to the environment (aka not listening) or dazed behaviour (freeze). When one or more of these behaviours are exhibited by the child, the adult in a care and management role might respond with anger and admonish the child, thereby (albeit inadvertently) confirming and strengthening the idea/belief that they are about to be hurt, feelings of being unsafe and the necessity of engaging in self-protective behaviours associated with the fight-flight-freeze response. I have represented this process in Figure 3.6.

Figure 3.6 An example of how a thought becomes a belief

We can circumvent this cycle, thereby preventing unhelpful ideas from becoming unhelpful beliefs, or weakening the power of existing unhelpful beliefs, by changing the way in which we respond to the child's behaviour – by responding with understanding (Figure 3.7).

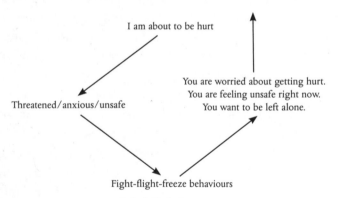

Figure 3.7 Circumventing unhelpful beliefs

When you respond with understanding, the child experiences relief and a sense that you can be trusted, both of which disconfirm the original thought, thereby weakening the influence of negativistic and unhelpful thinking associated with disordered attachment representations.

Keeping with this theme of enriching the child's experience that you understand them, a second aspect of conventional caregiving that is key to enriching the child's experience of having consistent access to a responsive adult caregiver involves maintaining the thought that *nobody does anything for no reason*. As I have already discussed, children who have an attachment disorder are inordinately preoccupied with needs that, historically, were met on an inconsistent basis, or not at all. Under such circumstances, these children will have learnt that in order to reassure themselves that they will have access to important needs provision they need to engage in behaviours that secure needs provision at a high rate and with great persistence. They are demanding and/or inordinately self-reliant. Their persistent behaviour to satisfy a need is not usefully dismissed as naughty behaviour, and ignored or disciplined. For the child who has an attachment disorder this type of response will only create further uncertainty that their needs are understood and important and will be addressed through conventional caregiving from a consistently responsive caregiver. Worse still are measures instituted to further restrict the child's access to needs provision, such as locks on fridges and cupboards to guard against the child eating you out of house and home. This will only further exacerbate their preoccupations and associated demanding and deceitful behaviour. Rather, it is vital that you see the behaviour as the child's way of satisfying a need that was responded to inconsistently or not at all when they were an infant, and *respond to the need as well as the behaviour*. This means that for the child who interrupts your conversations, your trips to the bathroom and even your sleep, you need to acknowledge and respond to their need for attention. It also means that for the child who is constantly hanging around the kitchen, you need to offer them food and drink. It further means that the child who is controlling, aggressive, destructive and/or prone to running and hiding and/or freezing and dazed behaviour needs to be offered experiences that make them feel safe. Additional examples are offered in Table 3.2.

Table 3.2 Responding to the need as well as the behaviour

Behaviour	Possible explanation	Need	Helpful responses	Unhelpful responses
Child refuses to stay in their bed at night time	Separation anxiety and/or insecurity	Reassurance that the caregiver is aware of them, accessible and responsive	Remain calm Engage in soothing bedtime rituals (e.g. reading and singing to child) Checking back in with the child before they get out of bed to achieve physical closeness to the caregiver	Parental anger and frustration Disciplining the child Ignoring the child
Child refuses to eat their food	Child does not like the taste of the food or its texture (i.e. they may be tactile sensitive)	Food that is nutritious, tastes good and feels good on the palate	Remain calm Prepare nutritious meals that are to the child's taste Seek advice from an occupational therapist who specialises in sensory integration difficulties and a dietician who specialises in children's diet	Parental anger and frustration Making the child remain seated until they have eaten all of the food Threats and consequences for noncompliance
Child becomes overly loud and boisterous at a family function	Child is overstimulated	Soothing and/ or opportunities to blow off steam	Temporarily withdrawing the child from the stimulating environment in order to calm/soothe them or provide them with a release	Yelling at the child to 'calm down'
Child 'shuts down' in class	Child is overstimulated	Reduce stress	Understanding and soothing	Threatening and punishing

Now, some of you will be thinking *I am not rewarding naughty or unwanted behaviour* or *we will create a tyrant!* I have sympathy for this concern and, in order to address this, I think we need to return to the work of Skinner. Remember, the animals in Skinner's experiments that had received food inconsistently for presses of the lever when first placed in the Skinner Box continued to press the lever with high rate and great persistence after they received food for every press of the lever; that is, when conditions changed and they were in a consistently rewarding (think responsive) environment. Remember the other animals that were initially not rewarded at all for presses of the bar or lever. Moving to a consistent reinforcement condition made no impact on them either. So, how do we undo the unhelpful learning of both groups? We put the food in a bowl in the cage. We respond to the need proactively, before the animal does anything to make it so.

Similarly, with children who have an attachment disorder and a history of gross deficiencies in their consistent access to a responsive caregiver, we must consider their behaviour (be it demanding or self-reliant) and what needs they are drawing attention to and address those needs before they do anything to secure access to their needs. Only then will they have the experience that their needs are understood and important and will be responded to through an adult offering conventional care. In doing so we further undermine unhelpful thoughts about their own lack of deservedness and the lack of responsiveness of adult caretakers and promote the alternate, helpful attachment representations associated with attachment security:

- 'I am a good and deserving person.'

- 'My caregiver understands me and is responsive to my needs.'

- 'The world is a satisfying and safe place.'

In Table 3.3 I offer examples of proactive needs provision.

Table 3.3 Proactive needs provision

Behaviour	Need	Proactive needs provision
Child hoards food	Reassurance that they will always have access to food	Make healthy snacks, such as fruit, available all the time
Child is hostile and aggressive Child avoids others Child repeatedly attempts to leave the classroom/school	To feel safe	Verbalise understanding Facilitate engagement in activities where they experience a sense of mastery Offer roles (e.g. class monitor) where they have a sense of being able to influence their world in a structured and agreed way
Child breaks their toys	To feel safe from exploitation by others	Provide a place for the secure storage of toys and treasured items
Child refuses to go/stay in bed	To maintain connection To feel safe	Extended bedtime ritual For a simple method for getting children to sleep see below
Child repeatedly calls out in class	To reassure themselves that you are accessible and will be responsive	Offer them attention before they do anything to gain it

A simple method for getting children off to sleep

In my practice one of the more common struggles reported by parents and caregivers is getting children off to sleep in their own bed. What follows is a simple method to address this issue, which I often recommend and which I used with my own children.

Before I get to the method, I want to advise that there are many and varied reasons why children have difficulty getting off to sleep in their own bed. Time and space do not permit me to go into all possible reasons here. What I would say is that the method presented here is appropriate for many of the reasons why children have this difficulty. It is offered as general advice and is not a substitute for a full assessment and recommendation from an appropriately qualified paediatric sleep specialist.

First, children's sleep patterns are subject to a sleep–wake cycle, which is physiological in nature but strongly influenced by bedtime and wake-time routines. A stable and consistent bedtime and wake-time are important for establishing a stable sleep–wake cycle. That's right, a stable wake-time is just as important as a stable bedtime. If your child is having difficulty getting off to sleep, don't let them sleep in. Wake them up at a consistent time every day, regardless of how long it took them to go to sleep. Their wake-time should usually be approximately 10–12 hours after their bedtime.

The sleep–wake cycle is also affected by exposure to light and its impact on melatonin production. Melatonin production is implicated in the onset of sleep. Light is thought to suppress melatonin production. So, ensure that your child is in a light-reduced environment for at least 30 minutes before their bedtime. If your child requires a night light, use an orange one, as it has been suggested that orange light does not suppress melatonin production as much as other forms of light.

Now, once it is bedtime, I suggest that you put your child to bed and sit or lay alongside them for approximately 20 minutes. In that time, you should read to them and sing them lullabies. Read first and then sing. As with other aspects of parenting and caregiving, consistency is important here. I suggest rotating through a small number of books and a small number of lullabies across consecutive nights. Children draw comfort from the predictability of the bedtime routine, thus preparing them for the separation involved in going to sleep. After a while, the lullabies are likely to become associated with feelings of sleepiness, with the result that the child begins to feel sleepy when the same lullabies are sung to them.

If your child falls asleep during the above, you are free to leave the room. If they are still awake, you move to the next stage of the method. This involves providing the profound reassurance the child requires to cope with separation and go to sleep. If it works, it will circumvent the child's effort to engage in proximity-seeking behaviour, such as calling out, getting out of bed, searching for you, complaining of having a tummy ache, asking to go to the toilet and so on.

After you have read and sung to your child, say to them something like 'I am just going to put the light on in the next room and I will be right back. You can stay awake until I come back.' Then, you literally walk out of the room and walk back in almost straight away. You acknowledge that the child is okay and then say 'I am just going to put the kettle on and I will be straight back. You can stay awake until I come back.' You then do this and when you return to the child you say something like 'I am just going to the toilet and I will be straight back. You can stay awake until I come back.' You then do this and when you return to the child you say something like 'I am just going to have my cup of tea and I will be straight back. You can stay awake until I come back.' With each separation, you tell the child that you are doing an activity that takes longer and longer to complete. You keep doing this until, when you return to the child, you find them to be asleep.

Speaking of activities that have temporal (i.e. time) meaning is more easily understood by the child than saying 'I'll be back in a minute.' Choosing longer and longer activities involves exposing children gradually to separations, such that they do not become overly anxious, call out or get out of bed. It is important to return to the child before they call out or get out of bed, because parent-initiated proximity is more reassuring than child-initiated proximity. So adjust the separation as required to ensure that you get back to them before they leave their bed to find you! Telling the child to stay awake is an important way to circumvent potential conflict and associated parental frustration, with the result that the child is calmer and more likely to fall asleep. Put in a different way, this is a useful way of making use of 'Reverse Psychology'.

Playing relaxing classical music softly in the child's bedroom is a useful adjunct to the above. Finally, enjoy this special time spent with your child. I did, and experienced sadness when my youngest said 'Dad, I don't need you to stay with me anymore.'

Organising need-seeking behaviour

For particularly preoccupied and demanding children, a token system represents a methodology for organising the child's attempts to secure needs provision under conditions where the child's caregivers will be anticipating and responding to the child's usual daily needs proactively. It involves providing the child with a finite number of tokens each day and explaining to the child that each time they want the caring adult to attend and respond to a reasonable expressed need they need to hand the adult a token, where a reasonable expressed need would include the need for a snack, drink or the caregiver's involvement in an activity of the child's choosing and an unreasonable expressed need would include demands for inappropriate foods, new toys or the monopolisation of the caregiver's time. The amount of tokens given to a child depends on their age and neediness and the accessibility and likely responsiveness of the caring adult. Ten tokens may be sufficient for some children for the span of one full day with a caring adult. A smaller number may be sufficient for school-aged children during the school week. The caring adult should make certain that the child is only given sufficient tokens to ensure that the caring adult can respond to all reasonable requests presented in this way, either straight away or soon after the token is presented (the use of 'Yes, when…' can be useful in regard to the latter). It is permissible to respond to other needs that the child has without the presentation of the token, where it is the adult who anticipates and initiates needs provision (e.g. the need for three main meals per day and the need to go to sleep in the evening). When the tokens run out, the caring adult should continue to respond to basic needs (e.g. food, warmth, protection) and reassure the child regarding this. The caring adult should remind the child to use their tokens wisely before they use them all in a given day. In the face of persistent demands, the caring adult may say to the child something like: 'That is something I would do anyway; do you really want to use a token for that?' After the first week, the number of tokens can be reduced slightly, and again after each week thereafter. After not less than two weeks, expressed needs communicated in a socially sanctioned manner can be responded to once all the child's tokens have been exhausted. That is, the caregiver should continue to respond to a reasonable expressed need after their daily allocation of tokens has been exhausted in order to reinforce appropriate needs expression. However, if the child becomes overwhelmingly demanding again, the caring adult should consider re-instituting the token system from the beginning.

In the writer's experience, children who have an attachment disorder attempt to ensure that their tokens last an entire day, thus providing the caring adult with welcome relief from constant demands. Children who have an attachment disorder become less demanding because the presence of tokens is reassuring to them. They have a system by which they can consistently and successfully access needs provision. In addition, the system encourages the development and use of socially sanctioned expression of needs. To the extent that the system engenders consistent sensitive responsiveness from caring adults, reduces antisocial behaviour and reassures the child, the twin goals of reducing arousal and promoting positive attachment representations are promoted.

When the request is reasonable but the timing is poor, don't say 'no', say 'yes, when...'

Conventional wisdom suggests that children need to accommodate the refusal of some of their requests. That is, they need to hear 'no'. Nevertheless, they also need to hear 'yes' and have their requests responded to and validated. Demanding children may make many requests of their caregivers and become increasingly demanding, unsettled and alienated in association with frequent rejection of their wishes. Children who have an attachment disorder often experience exaggerated feelings of rejection in association with hearing 'no'. Both groups of children may defiantly do what they please in anticipation of a negative parental response, resulting in loss of parental authority and disruption to caregiver–child relationships. Saying 'yes, when...' avoids a confrontation, reinforces caregiver authority and promotes a more positive perception of caregiver understanding and responsiveness. It is also a useful strategy for getting children to perform required chores (e.g. 'Yes, you can go next door to play when you have dried the dishes.'). Furthermore, it avoids a perception of parental inconsistency and reinforcing persistent demanding behaviour, which can arise in the context of caring adults initially saying 'no' and later saying 'yes' in response to persistent demanding.

Emotional connectedness

The final component of the CARE model discussed in this book is emotional connectedness. Emotional connectedness is something that has been experienced inconsistently or not at all by the child who has an attachment disorder. Their distress has been relieved inconsistently or not at all, resulting in a proneness to hyperarousal and emotion-driven behaviours. In some instances, their caregiver has been the source of their distress. They have not known, or not known consistently enough to trust in it, the experience of an emotional union with another person; one that promotes an appreciation of the experience of others and the foundations for a capacity for empathy, emotional reciprocity and co-regulation. They have not felt heard on an emotional level. They have not experienced validation.

Children who have an attachment disorder benefit from enriched experiences of emotional connectedness, though they may initially be defensive about it. Remember, their first care experiences were ones where their emotions were not acknowledged consistently and by a consistent, accessible and responsive adult. At other times their first caregivers were the source of the child's distress. As a result, the child who has an attachment disorder often shows avoidance of intimacy and shared emotional experience. They are defensive about it. This leaves them cut off from meaningful experiences of connection with others that promotes not only the experience of feeling heard and cared for by others, but also an awareness of the experience of others and of the requirement to control and regulate their behaviour in order to remain on good terms with others – a process known as socio-emotional reciprocity or the give-and-take in relationships. Being emotionally distant from others, they are also cut off from the influence of a stable and empathic emotional connection with an adult in a caregiving role who can help them to regulate their emotions and behaviours.

In order to assist the child who has an attachment disorder to overcome their defensiveness about maintaining an emotional connection with others we need to maintain a connection with them. There are two traps that caregivers often fall into – one is to connect too deeply and too quickly, and the other is to respond to the emotional expressions of the child through deadpanning (where deadpanning refers to the caregiver offering the child no observable emotional response). With regard to the latter, deadpanning is not useful because it represents a break in emotional connection. Where it is recommended, it is generally couched in explanations that it does not further heighten the emotional state of the child, but I would counter that it leaves the child feeling misunderstood, with the result that their distress and maladaptive perceptions of human connection are reinforced and strengthened. In evidence of this, I would remind the reader of the results of the still-face experiments referred to in Chapter 1.

At other times, well-meaning caregivers attempt to compensate for all the love and positive regard that the child who has an attachment disorder has been denied during their early development. This can have the unfortunate result of starting a kind of emotional rollercoaster, whereby the child with the attachment disorder experiences the expressed emotion of the caregiver as overwhelming, thus activating their defences and associated hostile and distancing behaviour, only for the child to then become concerned about the carer being too distant and, hence, unavailable as a source of needs provision. The result is they seek to reengage the carer through a charm offensive, only to feel overwhelmed again when the carer responds with renewed effort to compensate for all the love and positive regard that the child has missed out on.

A more effective way to make and sustain a meaningful and therapeutic emotional connection to the child who has an attachment disorder is to observe the situation, the child's behaviour and any outward displays of emotion and allow yourself to feel what they are feeling. Open yourself to your instinctive empathic response; that one where you cannot help laughing at the unbridled mirth of the laughing baby or stop the welling of tears when confronted with the distress of another. Express your instinctive empathic response, though in a measured way, so as to not overwhelm the child who has an attachment disorder and activate their defensive avoidance. Return to calm. They will follow via a curious process by which once we have established an emotional connection to another, we tend to be drawn in to following the emotions of the other, wherever they lead. And children who have an attachment disorder are particularly sensitive and sensitised to the emotions of others and the emotional tone of their environment.[62]

This is a particularly useful adjunct to verbalising understanding and proactive needs provision. It amplifies the power of the experience of understanding for the child by providing them with the experience that not only are they heard in what you say (verbalising understanding) and what you do (proactive needs provision), but they are also understood in what you express. My recommendation is that in addition to what you say and what you do, you match your emotional expressions to the emotional experience of the child. You say and do it *with feeling*. Begin in a measured way and, in time, they will tolerate you being enthusiastic and demonstrative.

Putting it all together – a game of Uno®

As the name of this book implies, this is a short introduction to attachment and attachment disorder. It is beyond the scope of the book to offer extensive explanations and case examples for the ideas contained herein and the strategies introduced in this chapter. For readers who are seeking more extensive information and coaching regarding therapeutic approaches to the care and management of children who are recovering from gross deficiencies in their early CARE and the care of those who do the caregiving I would draw their attention to the Triple-A Model of Therapeutic Care. Triple-A, for short, is a step-by-step therapeutic approach to the care of children who are recovering from abuse and neglect, and their caregivers. It draws on much of the material and strategies from this book and offers further coaching and advice about establishing a therapeutic care environment and therapeutic care and relational strategies. Triple-A has been implemented in Ireland and Australia, but is available for implementation internationally. For more information about Triple-A I would refer the reader to my website.[63]

It would not have escaped your notice that in the preceding paragraph I referred to the care of those who care for children recovering from gross deficiencies in their early care arrangements. I cannot emphasise enough how important this is. It is a sad irony of working with children who have an attachment disorder and other difficulties arising from their early experience of gross deficiencies in CARE that as they appear to get better, their carers' functioning often declines. Vicarious trauma, secondary traumatisation and compassion fatigue are all salient aspects of the experience of adults whose role it is to care for these deeply hurt and troubled children. They challenge their caregivers, often to and beyond breaking point, leaving their carers doubting themselves, their competencies and even their sanity. The child's known history is distressing enough, and for many it triggers the caregiver's own history of hurt and loss, as does the child's behaviour. Caregivers themselves benefit from an enriched experience of support and understanding and being empowered to make a positive change in the lives of the children in their care, thereby achieving a sense of personal competence and mastery. For, without carers for these children, all endeavours to safeguard the best interests of children are compromised.

So, I do not wish to overwhelm you. The role you are performing is already a difficult one. You may say that you have little or no time or opportunity to implement the strategies contained in this chapter. I hear you. I expect you are thinking a 'but' is coming. Well, let's say I want to introduce you to a very simple first step in implementing the ideas and strategies contained in this book. Remember, I only want you to do what you can maintain over time. It is counter-productive to make and begin to implement grand plans, only to abandon them in a short while in the face of relentless defensive behaviour from the child you are caring for and managing.

My simple first step involves the card game Uno®. I choose to use Uno®, though there are many other games involving normal playing cards that work just as well for what I am about to recommend. Uno® is a card game where players contest with each other to be the first to dispose of all of their cards. There are ups and downs in the game. There is a winner and a loser(s). A typical hand takes less than five minutes to play. So here is the strategy. Schedule in a game of Uno® with the child who has an attachment disorder at a time and with a frequency that you can maintain over time. Remember the 'C' in CARE – consistency. Only set out to do what you can consistently maintain over time. It you are a parent, you might set aside some time between the evening meal and bedtime. If you are a teacher, you might schedule some time during a break from your direct teaching role or during a scheduled break. It is vital that the game is implemented consistently.

Be sure that you schedule the game at a time when the child is your sole focus and you are free from distractions. This, together with a consistent regime, will satisfy the second component of CARE – that you are accessible to the child. Make it a ritual between you and the child. Next, I want you to play the hand the child has. What do I mean? I mean you need to inhibit your comments and emotional reactions to the ups and downs of the game associated with your own cards and make comments and express emotions that are consistent with the hand the child has been dealt and their own experience of the game. When they play a good card, you say *that feels good* or *that will teach me for playing a mean card against you*. When they have to pick up extra cards because of a card you have played, you watch them closely and say what you think is going through their mind, such as *oohhh drats*. More than this, you match your own outward emotion to that of the child and you *say it with feeling*. As I said, you play their hand and their associated experiences during the game. In doing so, you satisfy the third and fourth components of CARE – responsiveness and emotional connectedness. Finally, when they win, you are happy. If they lose, you are disappointed. Try not to let them lose too often. They have already lost so much in their life.

BE ALL POWERFUL, ALL UNDERSTANDING, ALL KNOWING!

An attachment figure is a person the child goes to when they are sick, sad, hurt or scared. They are the person whom the child perceives to be better able to cope with circumstances that are painful, stressful or frightening. They are a source of comfort and protection for the child. In order to be an attachment figure and a source of comfort, support and protection for the child, a caregiver needs to be seen by the child as being more powerful, more knowing and more understanding than the child. From the child's perspective, such a strong person can protect the child in all circumstances. If a child is allowed to be the boss, they will never feel truly secure. Similarly, if a child has no boundaries or expectations placed upon them by an authoritative adult, they will think that adults do not care.

One approach that casts the adult in an all-knowing role and facilitates the child's acceptance of adult authority is teaching the child a new game or activity. Introducing a controlling and otherwise difficult child to a fun or interesting new activity and teaching them how to do it creates an often unique situation where the child who has an attachment disorder will accept adult authority and direction in association with being motivated to learn the desired activity or game (e.g. chess). In addition, if the activity is fun as well, the child experiences pleasure in association with learning and accepting direction from a caring adult. With repeated exposure to such experiences, the child instinctively experiences pleasure and other desirable feelings in association with adults being in charge and teaching them. Psychologists refer to this process as *Classical Conditioning* and the response engendered by a particular stimulus as a *Conditioned Response*. It is possible that the desirable Conditioned Response will generalise to other aspects of the child's life where they experience the adult in an authoritative role.

Play is also important in the remediation (e.g. amelioration) of attachment disorders for other reasons. Play:

- offers opportunity for attunement experiences
- promotes positive conceptions of self and other

- allows the adult to structure and organise the behaviour and affective displays of the child in a nonthreatening manner.

Where a child is likely to be contrary, you wish to direct them regarding your wishes, and their compliance is non-negotiable, do not ask the child, *tell* the child. If you ask them, you are effectively giving them a choice regarding whether to comply or not. If they say 'no', you are in a lose–lose situation, in that they either do not do what you expect of them or you precipitate a confrontation that can have the effect of upsetting and alienating the child.

Children respond better to directions and outcomes rather than to directions and punishments, for example 'Pick up your toys and you can go out and play', rather than 'Pick up your toys or you're grounded.' Nevertheless, where children remain defiant and discipline is warranted, express empathy for the child's feelings, but follow through with directions or consequences. Don't allow the child to maintain an emotional tone of anger and hostility.

In association with their experience of unreliable and unresponsive parenting, children who have an attachment disorder learn that the only person they can rely on is themselves. This often manifests as an intense need to control their environment and everything in it, including the thoughts, feelings and behaviours of others, a goal they achieve through naughty, coercive/manipulative behaviour. A power struggle can often ensue when the child's caregiver attempts to assert normal adult authority and direct the child. Children who have an attachment disorder often enjoy engaging in power struggles and experience a compulsion to win them. Borrowing from principles implicit in martial arts, the push–pull approach uses the child's intense desire for control to reinforce adult authority. This is achieved when, rather than directing a child regarding inconsequential (to the adult) matters (e.g. which breakfast cereal to eat, which shirt to wear, which TV programme to watch during TV time), an adult caregiver offers the child choices and reinforces that they can make this decision. This strategy meets the child's need for control while also reinforcing the adult's authority through the offering of choices.

Finally, *Paradoxical Intention*, or *Reverse Psychology* as it is more commonly referred to, is a particularly effective short-term strategy for circumventing attempts made by the child who has an attachment disorder to regulate the emotional closeness of caring adults through affective displays and, hence, facilitates adult influence over this important aspect of the relationship. For instance, some children who have an attachment disorder have a tendency to frown and project an outward attitude of hostility or anger in an attempt to distance caring adults. Under such circumstances, I verbalise to the child that they are right to frown and/or look serious, sad or angry, as this is a serious, sad or frustrating time. Furthermore, they are right to not smile. Invariably the child starts to smile. The caring adult should playfully remind them that this is a serious, sad or frustrating time and smiling is not appropriate. The child will then seek to stop smiling, only to burst into laughter. The caring adult should state that it is certainly not a time for laughter. By this time the serious, sad or angry child is in an emotional state fit for meaningful engagement.

ADDITIONAL CONSIDERATIONS

The care requirements of children who have an attachment disorder are significant and yet parental care alone may not be sufficient to promote the development of, and adherence to, secure attachment representations in these children. Children who have an attachment disorder require intervention at the environmental (home and school) and individual levels.

Psychotherapy is an important component of the remediation of their attachment problems. Caregivers and teachers of these children also benefit from psychoeducation from practitioners specialised in providing advice regarding the care of these children. Hence, the involvement of a knowledgeable psychotherapist is generally a requirement.

CHAPTER SUMMARY

- The remediation of attachment disorders promotes individual happiness and the welfare and wellbeing of the community as a whole.

- We need to offer experiences of enriched CARE to children who have an attachment disorder. Enriched CARE, particularly where it confines itself to conventional care and management behaviours, represents the best hope of subtly challenging and sneaking through the carefully tended defences of the child who has an attachment disorder.

- Through enriched CARE we stand the best chance of promoting attachment security, reducing arousal and associated anxiety proneness and facilitating new learning that the needs of children who have an attachment disorder are understood and important and will be responded to through conventional care and without them having to go to great lengths to make it so.

- Consistency is the essential precondition for success in all of our endeavours to assist children who have an attachment disorder. Whatever we do, we must do it consistently.

- When you orient to children who have an attachment disorder proactively, they will experience that you are accessible and interested in them and that they are worthy and deserving of the same.

- Enriching responsiveness requires that caregivers do three things – hold appropriate developmental expectations, communicate understanding of the child's thoughts, feelings, intentions and needs and address those needs proactively.

- Children who have an attachment disorder benefit from enriched experiences of emotional connectedness, though they may initially be defensive about it. In order to assist the child who has an attachment disorder to overcome their defensiveness about maintaining an emotional connection with others we need to maintain a connection with them, as opposed to cycling through states of emotional closeness and distance.

- Children who have an attachment disorder require intervention at the environmental (home and school) and individual levels. Psychotherapy is an important component of the remediation of their attachment problems. Caregivers and teachers of these children also benefit from psychoeducation from practitioners specialised in providing advice regarding the care of these children.

MATTHEW'S STORY CONTINUED

During the initial consultation with Matthew's foster parent, Helen, she reported that she had read numerous books on traumatised and attachment-disordered children and obtained information off the internet, but that nothing she did to manage Matthew's behaviour seemed to work consistently. In fact, she described a pattern whereby she would try something new, it would work for a while, it would start to lose its effectiveness and she would be forced to try a new strategy or approach. One intervention approach that consistently did not work was behaviour management. In particular, sending Matthew to his room for time-out precipitated a dramatic deterioration in his emotional state and behaviour. Withdrawal of prized items and privileges from Matthew only appeared to increase his resentment, notwithstanding the fact that he would state 'don't care' as the last of his toys were being taken from his room. She concluded that love was not enough for a child like Matthew and that he was not particularly lovable anyway. She acknowledged feeling like a failure.

In response to the above, the psychologist advised Helen that maintaining a consistent approach to his care and management was important. As tactfully as could be achieved, he explained that repeated changes in management approach created an inconsistent care environment that was itself unsettling for Matthew. He advocated the implementation and maintenance of a small number of strategies known to address accessibility preoccupations, negative beliefs about self and other and hyperarousal/ anxiety. He reassured Helen that these approaches were part of reflective conventional caregiving and relationship behaviour and, hence, represented fine-tuning of parenting rather than a radically different approach. He acknowledged that Matthew's behaviour might get worse before it got better as he coercively attempted to reinstitute Helen's usual pattern of relating to him. He explained that Matthew's behaviour in this regard represented his own attempts to reassure himself that his beliefs about how his world worked were still valid. He advised that an important component of parenting approaches that would be recommended was that they would increase Helen's influence in the relationship with Matthew. He explained that only through Matthew experiencing her as understanding of, and responsive to, his needs would Matthew relinquish his controlling and self-reliant behaviour and depend increasingly on her. He also advised that Matthew would benefit from teaching staff at his school implementing a similar care and management approach and advised how it is his usual practice to approach the school and offer some general training to all school staff regarding key aspects of the care and management of a child who has an attachment disorder, with follow-up interactions with key personnel regarding more specific strategies.

With regard to Helen's own feelings of self-doubt, the psychologist reassured her that this was a common occurrence for caregivers of children who have an attachment disorder. The psychologist explored aspects of Helen's conventional caregiving that were good examples of CARE, such as when she offered Matthew something to eat at school pick-up, when she felt sad and frustrated for Matthew when he could not do his school homework and when she checked in on him to let her know where she would be when she went into the back garden to hang out the laundry. The psychologist reassured Helen that each of these were good examples of the CARE experiences Matthew required to achieve attachment security. Feeling validated in her endeavours, Helen allowed herself to trust that the psychologist would be of assistance to both her and Matthew. She opened up further about her approach to caregiving. The psychologist identified further ways in which Helen offered sound CARE experiences to Matthew and offered guidance regarding how these could be extended and implemented consistently. Having felt heard by the psychologist, Helen felt prepared to accept the psychologist's feedback and guidance.

Over the ensuing weeks the psychologist met regularly with Helen, either after one of Matthew's scheduled sessions or separately from them. During these meetings the psychologist engaged in further fine-tuning of Helen's caregiving, particularly in the use of verbalising understanding. Over the ensuing weeks, Helen reported that Matthew was calmer, less demanding and more inclined to express his needs verbally. However, approximately three months after the intervention commenced Helen reported that Matthew was becoming unsettled and unreasonably demanding and controlling again, such that she was again feeling dispirited and defeated. The psychologist reassured her that such setbacks were expected. He explained that, as she became emotionally closer to Matthew and he valued their relationship, Matthew would experience stronger feelings of shame associated with minor misdemeanours and seek to withdraw from engagement with, and dependency on, others as a defence against experiencing this powerful aversive emotion. The psychologist advised Helen that, more than ever, Matthew needed to be reassured that she would go on caring for him no matter what misbehaviour he engaged in by maintaining the enriched approach to CARE, incorporating additional experiences for Matthew of understanding and reassurance regarding his feelings of shame.

CHAPTER 4

TREATING ATTACHMENT INSECURITY AND DISORDER

Fundamental Requirements for Effective Treatment

In this chapter I will present what I consider to be the fundamental requirements for treating children who have an attachment disorder and promoting attachment security in an ethical and effective manner. In doing so I will draw on diverse contributions to my thinking, including my initial training in clinical psychology, my subsequent professional development, my experience of treating children over more than 20 years and my reflections about all of these things. I will confine myself to that which is generally accepted as good practice in the psychology profession and that which is derived from theories and practices that have an evidence base. The presentation of a specific evidence-based approach or approaches that have been tailored to the treatment of children who have an attachment disorder relies, somewhat, on there emerging a greater interest in the academic community in disorders of attachment and the development of scientifically tested, evidence-based treatments.

First and foremost, children who have an attachment disorder require therapeutic care and management. That is, they require adults in a care and management role in the home and education settings to be implementing therapeutic care principles and practices, such as those that were presented in Chapter 3. It is vital that they are implementing the same or very similar therapeutic care principles and practices, as consistency of the child's experience of care across environments is critical to any endeavour to achieve the goal of healthy attachment outcomes. It is also generally necessary that they are guided by a skilled therapist who has expertise in intervening with disorders of attachment, and that there is consistency between what is occurring in face-to-face treatment between the child and the therapist and the child's experience of relating to adults in a care and management role outside of the therapeutic consulting room. Where there is inconsistency, endeavours to assist children who have an attachment disorder are compromised by an inadvertent re-enactment of the inconsistency in care and management that was a feature of their first care environments. Remember, *consistency* is the key.

Schools play a critical role in a child's recovery from an attachment disorder. Schools are such a significant part of the life of any child. Children who have an attachment disorder are a significant care and management challenge in any school and a significant drain on school resources.[64, 65, 66] Successful management of children who have an attachment disorder in the school environment benefits the whole school community. There appears to be three types of school culture and two types of teacher. Dealing first with school culture, the first kind is disinterested in advice proffered by an external treating professional regarding the care and management of children who have an attachment disorder. The second type of school culture is one where there is interest in what an external treating professional has to say, but little follow-through with proffered guidance regarding the care and management of children who have an attachment disorder. The third type of school culture is one where there is both interest in what an external professional has to say and implementation of the proffered advice and guidance regarding the care and management of the child who has an attachment disorder. With regard to teachers, there are teachers who see their role as educators alone, and there are those who also see themselves as caregivers as well as educators. It seems obvious to say, but the optimal school environment for the child who has an attachment disorder is one where the school culture is accepting of advice and guidance from an external treating professional who has expertise in the care and management of children who have an attachment disorder, implements this advice and employs teaching staff who see themselves as caregivers as well as educators.

There is individual variability among the caregivers of children who have an attachment disorder, just as there is variability in care arrangements. Many children who have an attachment disorder are in stable, long-term, foster, adoptive or kinship care placements. Others are in residential care environments, where they are cared for by rotating shifts of residential care workers. Still others are in emergency care environments where they are cared for by rotating shifts of paid carers (e.g. nannies). Many move between different care placements and different types of care placement. Of critical importance to endeavours to treat children who have an attachment disorder is the need to achieve consistency between carers and between the different types of care environment. This is where training in, and implementation of, broad-based therapeutic models of care is particularly useful, such as in the CARE-based practices described in Chapter 3 or the Triple-A Model of Therapeutic Care, each of which offer practical care and relational strategies that can be implemented in the home and the classroom environment.

There also needs to be consistency of therapist and therapeutic approach. Treatment with children who have an attachment disorder is rarely a short-term endeavour. It is also relational. The therapist takes on a kind of parental role. One of the goals of treatment is for the children to make and maintain a healthy relationship with their treating therapist. The therapeutic relationship becomes a model or template for secure relatedness to others outside of the consulting room. It follows that it is counter-productive to undertake the vital role of primary therapist to the child who has an attachment disorder if you cannot see it through to the end. This often requires persistence in the face of the child's endeavours to test the therapist's commitment to them and to reject and distance them. Under such circumstances the therapist may question whether their approach is working. If the child is reacting to the therapeutic approach with hostile and distancing behaviours, then the therapist is making an impression on the child. It would be counter-productive to change therapists and/or therapeutic approach, just as it is counter-productive to change alternate care placement or school placement because the child is engaging in hostile and/or distancing behaviours. This is often the child's way of resisting the formation of a natural and healthy dependency relationship, about which they are anxious and defensive. They may also be testing you to see if you really are as caring and committed to them as you are endeavouring to be. The most therapeutic thing to do in these circumstances is to hang in there with the child until they understand that you are not going to hurt or reject them. Changes in therapist and/or therapeutic approach, like changes in care arrangements or changes in school placement, re-enact the inconsistency and unpredictability that was a feature of the child's early life experiences and played a direct contributing role to their attachment disorder status.

My preceding comments are predicated on the type of care being offered, and the treatment approach, being appropriate to children who have an attachment disorder. In Chapter 3 I presented care and management practices that are appropriate to children who have an attachment disorder and which follow the CARE principles. What follows is a brief description of the therapeutic approach I utilise when working directly with these children, following the CARE principles.

CONSISTENCY

To begin with, I would like to reiterate and extend on a point made earlier. There needs to be consistency in approaches to care and management across environments and adults who interact with children who have an attachment disorder in a care and management role. Children who have an attachment disorder are inordinately prone to feeling anxious and the activation of defensive behaviours associated with the fight-flight-freeze response under conditions of inconsistency and unpredictability. The therapeutic approach adopted by the treating therapist needs to be consistent with what is being advocated for regarding care and management beyond the consulting room. Consider the experience of the child who experiences high levels of CARE in the consulting room, only to return to an (un)CARE(ing) environment outside of it. Children can feel resentful that the adults in a caregiving role in the home and education settings are not more like their therapist. The unfortunate outcome of this is increased hostility and maladaptive behaviour in the home and/or education settings.

I am not advocating here that the treatment approach needs to adapt itself to what is on offer to the child outside of the consulting room. Rather, I would emphasise the importance of a relational approach to treatment that can be extended to the child's experience of interacting with other key adults beyond the consulting room. The main difference is that treatment involves an intense and substantial dose of CARE.

Treatment involves a consistent approach and the consistent implementation of therapeutic techniques. The child should very soon know what to expect when they attend their treatment session. Treatment should incorporate repetition of certain activities, such that they become ritualised aspects of the treatment process, just as they experience rituals in the home (e.g. bedtime rituals) and at school (such as the study of reading, spelling and maths).

ACCESSIBILITY

Treatment should be implemented to a consistent schedule; one that the child can easily learn and have a sense of predictability about, just as they have with their home and education placement. My preference is for children to have a consistent appointment day and time each week, extending to each fortnight depending on the age and progress of the child in treatment. As mentioned earlier, there should be a primary treating therapist who is available for the long haul. Each of these arrangements facilitates the experience of the child that their therapist is accessible to them.

When they attend for treatment, children who have an attachment disorder need to have the experience that the therapist is there for them. Though they may attend with their caregiver, the child needs to experience that they are the first priority of the therapist. They might need to learn to wait at some point, but in the early stages of their treatment this is not the case. Rather, they need to learn that they are in the head and heart of others and that they are important and a priority, just as is the experience of the infant who is born into a stable and loving CARE environment. Children who have an attachment disorder either did not have these experiences or did not have them consistently, such that they doubt their worth and deservedness of attention and care. Learning to wait comes later in the development of every child, and the child who has an attachment disorder is no different.

So, notwithstanding that the promotion of a therapeutic CARE environment is an important task in any treatment endeavour, as far as is practicable, the child who has an attachment disorder is the first priority at treatment consultations. As far as possible, separate consultations should be scheduled with the caregivers of the child. Where caregivers are separately engaged with the child as part of the child's own consultation, care must be exercised to ensure that the child's concern about what is being discussed, and their likely feelings of shame, are addressed through acknowledgement of their concerns and the implementation of a separate arrangement to keep the child happily occupied while the adults engage with each other. Leaving a child who has an attachment disorder untended in the waiting room is not a suitable option.

RESPONSIVENESS

Just as in the approaches to CARE advocated in Chapter 3, treatment should offer the child an enriched experience that their thoughts, feelings, intentions and needs (also known as 'inner world') are understood and important and will be addressed proactively. In my preferred approach to the treatment of children who have an attachment disorder, there are no questions asked regarding their experience. Rather, the child is observed closely throughout the interaction and statements are made about their experience moment by moment. Many children refer to me as a 'mind-reader' and this is an outcome I am trying to achieve by *speaking their mind*. By speaking their mind, I am not only offering an enriched experience that their inner world is understood and important, I am also assisting them with words and a language framework for expressing themselves, thus reducing the need for the child who has an attachment disorder to communicate via their actions. It becomes increasingly difficult for the traumatised, attachment-disordered child to maintain beliefs that they are unsafe and unloved, and that others are harsh and uncaring, when they are safe, understood, cared for and delighted in through the medium of the therapeutic relationship. That is, the child's experience of the therapeutic relationship attains a central role in challenging maladaptive attachment representations and promoting adaptive alternatives.

Treatment is therapist-directed, just as the home is parent-directed and school is teacher-directed. It makes no sense for treatment to promote the belief that it should be otherwise for the child who has an attachment disorder. These children benefit from the experience that their therapist is in control of themselves, the environment and the interaction with the child. Though they may initially resist the therapist being in charge, as the therapeutic relationship develops and they learn that they can trust their therapist, the child will also be reassured that adults in a caregiving role do care about what the child does and are potent. A perception of the potency of adults facilitates beliefs that adults can be relied upon and will keep them safe from harm. Children feel safe when adults are in control of their own emotions and behaviour and of the interaction with the child. I calmly acknowledge the traumatised child's resistance to relinquishing control and attempts to punish and distance me in association with transferential processes, where such processes involve the child engaging with me as if I will be just the same as those who have afforded them inadequate care. I acknowledge the intent of their behaviour and affective displays. I verbalise understanding of the disordered attachment representations that subconsciously exert a powerful influence over the child's interactions with their self, others and their world. I *make statements* where others ask. I *direct* where others request cooperation and compliance. I offer *choices* where others argue. I am in control of myself, the interaction with the child and the therapeutic environment. I am successful because the child feels understood and validated. My consistent observation over many years of treating children who have an attachment disorder is that they respond to me taking charge with profound relief.

In treatment there is a focus on *process*, as opposed to *skills development*. Central to the *process* of my work is the provision of reparative attachment experiences. Treatment is experiential, just as early attachment relationships are formed through experiences. My intention is to create an environment and experiences where the child feels safe, validated, emotionally connected with, looked after and capable. Treatment involves enriched experiences that the child's needs are understood and important and will be addressed without the child having to control and regulate the therapist to make it so. I endeavour to provide a treatment environment and experiences where the child's need to feel safe, understood, accepted and physically and emotionally nourished are all addressed proactively by me. I am in charge, I communicate understanding, I do not judge the child, I share their highs and lows and I feed them.

EMOTIONAL CONNECTEDNESS

In my preferred approach to the treatment of children who have an attachment disorder, interaction is not just heard. It is not simply a process of one- or two-way conversation. Children who have an attachment disorder are often too young, or unable or unwilling, to engage in protracted two-way conversation in treatment and easily tune out from one-way conversation from the therapist. Rather, it is felt. Children who have an attachment disorder benefit from experiencing treatment on an emotional level. They benefit from treatment being fun as much as possible, as this ensures that they are a willing participant. If they are not a willing participant, it is difficult to conceive of them deriving any benefit from treatment. As children who have an attachment disorder typically exhibit a limited range of emotions associated with the fear and distress that marked their first care experiences, treatment should incorporate opportunities for diverse emotions. At all times the child must experience the therapist as being tuned in to their emotions. Child and therapist must be emotionally connected, allowing the therapist to not only lead the child through a range of emotional states, but also reduce the child's defensive avoidance of emotions by regularly and repeatedly restoring calm themselves and, in doing so, restoring calm for the child. Consequently, the child's own capacity to restore calm and maintain optimal arousal is promoted.

Incorporating play into treatment facilitates the child's willingness to attend and, thereby, their engagement in the treatment process. Play also facilitates opportunities for attunement experiences, where the child and I are experiencing the same or very similar emotions. This is important for providing the child with the experience of emotional connectedness with others that is often absent in their life. Experiences of emotional connectedness are implicated in the development of secure attachment relationships, as well as in the development of emotional (and arousal) self-regulation.[67, 68] As such, I utilise play as a means of facilitating a range of affective experience and a return to calm contentment.

Moreover, I utilise play as a means of providing the child with affirmative experiences, such that they experience themselves as likeable and capable, others as fun and nice and their world as safe and a source of happy experiences. In doing so, I am again seeking to challenge maladaptive attachment representations and promote adaptive alternatives.

OTHER CONSIDERATIONS

As I mentioned earlier in this chapter, there is a need for further endeavour to develop tailored and effective treatment approaches for children who have an attachment disorder. Independent of such endeavours, an ethical practitioner monitors progress of their client in treatment. In my own practice I ask the carers of the referred child to complete measures of pre-treatment functioning. Thereafter, and during the active phase of implementing a CARE approach in the home (and, if possible, the school) setting, I ask the carers of the child to complete daily/regular monitoring of behaviours we would expect to change. These behaviours relate to the goals of treatment, which include but are not limited to evidence of:

- the child's emerging sense of their worth
- the child communicating about their experience in words, as opposed to expressing their experience through behaviour
- the child depending on the caregiver for needs provision and accepting conventional caregiving
- the child maintaining lower arousal levels and less proneness to loss of emotional and behavioural control
- consistency between emotions and context

- increased social interest and willingness to engage in shared emotional experiences

- increased care about the impact of their behaviour on others and their relationship with others

- the child modifying their behaviour out of a concern for maintaining mutually satisfying relationships with others.

WHAT DO WE CALL THIS APPROACH TO TREATMENT?

This is an interesting question, as it contains elements of a number of evidence-based and evidence-informed treatment approaches. To some extent, it is in the eye of the beholder; that is, depending on people's primary treatment orientation they will see the elements that are consistent with their therapeutic orientation. I happily acknowledge that I draw heavily on Theraplay®[69] for therapeutic activities and to structure sessions. I am managing the child's implicit beliefs about relating to others (transference) and avoiding confirming them in my own response (counter-transference) by sustaining a deep and accepting connection to the child in the presence of their hostile and distancing behaviours. In this (and other) respects, the approach articulated in this chapter is psychodynamic. I am also attempting to raise to conscious awareness these implicit beliefs and challenge them through the child's experience of the therapeutic relationship, such that the approach is both psychodynamic and exposure-based. Combined with endeavours to challenge the child's maladaptive thinking and relational behaviours, and the promotion of new, optimal thinking and relational behaviours, my approach could easily be seen as cognitive-behavioural. This is supported by my primary therapeutic goal, the exposure of the child who has an attachment disorder to what they fear most – dependency on an adult caregiver – and promotion of reduced feelings of anxiety through sustained engagement and exposure to a caring adult. If I had to give it a name, I would call it Dynamic Attachment-Focused Cognitive-Behavioural Therapy.

CHAPTER SUMMARY

- Of critical importance to endeavours to treat children who have an attachment disorder is the need to achieve consistency between carers and between the different types of care environment.

- Children who have an attachment disorder require adults in a care and management role in the home and education settings to be implementing consistent therapeutic care principles and practices.

- It is generally necessary that caregivers in the home and education settings are guided by a skilled therapist who has expertise in intervening with disorders of attachment, and that there is consistency between what is occurring in face-to-face treatment between the child and the therapist and the child's experience of relating to adults in a care and management role outside of the therapeutic consulting room.

- Schools play a critical role in a child's recovery from an attachment disorder. The optimal school environment is one where the school culture is accepting of advice and guidance from an external treating professional who has expertise in the care and management of children who have an attachment disorder, implements this advice and employs teaching staff who see themselves as caregivers as well as educators.

- In treatment there is a focus on *process*, as opposed to *skills development*. Treatment is experiential, just as early attachment relationships are formed through experiences.

- There needs to be consistency of therapist and therapeutic approach. Changes in therapist and/or therapeutic approach, like changes in care arrangements or changes in school placement, re-enact the inconsistency and unpredictability that was a feature of the child's early life experiences and played a direct contributing role to their attachment disorder status.

- Treatment should be implemented to a consistent schedule, one that the child can easily learn and have a sense of predictability about.

- When they attend for treatment, children who have an attachment disorder need to have the experience that the therapist is there for them. Though they may attend with their caregiver, the child needs to experience that they are the first priority of the therapist.

- Treatment should offer the child an enriched experience that their thoughts, feelings, intentions and needs (also known as 'inner world') are understood and important and will be addressed proactively.

- Treatment is therapist-directed, just as the home is parent-directed and school is teacher-directed. It makes no sense for treatment to promote the belief that it should be otherwise for the child who has an attachment disorder.

- Treatment involves enriched experiences that the child's needs are understood and important and will be addressed without the child having to control and regulate the therapist to make it so.

- Children who have an attachment disorder are often too young, or unable or unwilling, to engage in protracted two-way conversation in treatment and easily tune out from one-way conversation from the therapist. Rather, it is felt. Children who have an attachment disorder benefit from experiencing treatment on an emotional level.

MATTHEW'S STORY CONTINUED

When Matthew attended for his first treatment session he was observed to be seated somewhat apart from his foster mother and wearing a scowl on his face. When greeted by the psychologist he averted his eyes and gave a minimal verbal response. The psychologist lowered himself to Matthew's eye-level and acknowledged, in tones of trepidation, Matthew's anxiety about attending his first consultation. The psychologist said *Oh, dear, you look like you don't want to be here.* In response, Matthew turned to the psychologist, made eye contact and simply stated 'Yeah,' to which the psychologist replied *You are not sure why you are being made to be here.* Again, Matthew muttered an affirmative response. The psychologist further stated *You probably think you were made to come because of something you did – something that you were told was bad.* By this stage Matthew was orienting to the psychologist and maintaining eye-to-eye-gaze. Matthew said nothing. The psychologist then stated *I know you did what you did for a reason. I am only interested in your reasons. But first, I am interested in having fun. So let's go and have some fun…*whereupon Matthew strode towards the psychologist's consulting room, as if he knew the way.

Once the psychologist caught up with Matthew and gave directions to the consulting room, Matthew stated 'I knew that.' Upon entering the psychologist's consulting room Matthew immediately went to the shelves where the games were kept, appearing to make a careful study of what was there. He began to handle the mini pool table. Noticing his interest, the psychologist commented that he could see that Matthew would like to have a game of pool. The psychologist advised Matthew that they would have a game of pool before the consultation was over. To reassure Matthew that this promise would not be forgotten the psychologist suggested that he and Matthew move the mini pool table to a prominent place in the centre of the room so that it could not be overlooked. Matthew confidently asserted that he could move it himself, and the psychologist commented *You like to do things yourself.* The psychologist directed Matthew regarding where he should place the mini pool table and then directed Matthew to a growth chart where the psychologist would add Matthew's name, with an explanation that they could check on how much Matthew had grown at the beginning of each visit thereafter.

When he arrived for his second treatment session Matthew was observed to be seated in the waiting room with an expectant expression. He greeted the psychologist before the psychologist had a chance to greet him. He set off to the consulting room prior to an invitation to do so. When the psychologist entered the consulting room he noted that Matthew was already setting up the mini pool table. The psychologist commented *You were not sure what would we would be doing today.* The psychologist reminded Matthew of the need to check his height against the measurement taken at the first session. Thereafter, the psychologist directed Matthew to remain standing while he took further measurements of Matthew's head circumference, ears, smile and muscles; on each occasion comparing Matthew's measurements to objects and aspects of the room (e.g. *Look, your brain is bigger than my computer; you are taller than the length of this table; your ears are the same size as your smile!*). Matthew was directed to continue to remain standing while the psychologist tested the extent to which his brain is the boss of his body by getting him to pop bubbles with the parts of his body identified by the psychologist, and tested his strength by breaking out of coloured streamers wrapped around his body.

When he arrived for the third session Matthew greeted the psychologist in a friendly manner and readily accompanied him to the consulting room. He remained close by the growth chart in anticipation of measurements being taken and responded with enthusiasm to exclamations regarding his growth. He confidently popped the bubbles as directed and asked for an additional streamer to be wrapped around him to demonstrate his growing strength. He was initially wary of the psychologist's advice that they would be doing a series of activities to test how lucky, clever and skilful he was and sought to hide in the play tent. In response to the psychologist's acknowledgement of his fears, Matthew engaged in the activities with increasing alacrity and in association with the psychologist mirroring his experience in words and outward emotion and manipulating the course of each activity to ensure that Matthew was ultimately successful. After the question of his cleverness, luckiness and skilfulness was apparently resolved through his experience of success in each activity, Matthew was happily declared to be *Cluckful*, in response to which he beamed!

In view of the care and management challenge Matthew was presenting at school, the psychologist's offer to consult with the school was accepted. On the day of the meeting the psychologist met with Matthew's classroom teacher and a senior staff member. The psychologist initially allowed the school staff to tell their story about their experiences of managing Matthew in the school environment and their associated concerns. The psychologist acknowledged their concerns and challenges and asked them what they were already doing to address these issues. On the basis of their answers, and in response to careful questioning and exploration, the psychologist identified those aspects of their care and management of Matthew that were consistent with good CARE. The psychologist made suggestions about how these aspects of CARE could be enriched in the school environment as part of the broader approach of enriching Matthew's experience of therapeutic CARE.

After six months of weekly treatment, Matthew confidently entered the psychologist's practice and greeted the reception staff in a friendly manner. He acknowledged positive comments about his clothes and enthusiastically drew attention to his new shoes and new haircut. He remained settled and polite in his interactions with his foster mother and reception staff and he waited patiently while the psychologist finished up and engaged in separation rituals with his previous client. He responded in kind to the psychologist's friendly greeting and readily responded to the writer's invitation to accompany him to the consulting room. As they left the reception, Matthew's foster mother could be heard to say *He just loves to come here.*

POSTSCRIPT

EYES ARE MIRRORS FOR A CHILD'S SOUL. WHAT DO CHILDREN SEE IN YOUR EYES?

In his 1902 publication, *Human Nature and the Social Order*, Charles Horton Cooley introduced the concept of the *Looking Glass Self* to portray his idea that an individual's perception of themselves develops in association with how they experience others seeing them. Using naturalistic observation as his primary research methodology, including observation of his own children, Cooley proposed that ideas of self incorporate:

- our thoughts about how we must appear to others

- our thoughts about the judgement of others of this appearance

- our feelings associated with the imagined judgements of others.

Empirical research has shown that how adolescents and young adults think of themselves is correlated with how they think they are perceived by their parents.[70] Though there is an emerging acknowledgement that, as they get older, individuals actively seek to influence the judgements of others, contemporary sociological research[71] lends support to the idea that 'self-conceptions are instilled through interaction with high-status [others]'. It follows that an individual's thoughts of how they must appear to others, their thoughts about the judgements of others of this appearance and the resultant feelings associated with the imagined judgements of others are likely to stem from the individual's experience of relatedness to others. Though not the sole determinant of self-concept, it is conceivable that if a child predominantly experiences significant others to be friendly and interested in them, understanding of them and accepting of who they are from an early age, the child will think of themselves as interesting, competent and approved of. In contrast, if a child predominantly experiences significant others to be inaccessible, frightening, rejecting or disinterested, they will think of themselves as bad, undeserving and unsafe. When one considers the historical experiences of children who have an attachment disorder, their maladjusted behaviour and the associated rejecting and punitive responses of adults in a caregiving role, it should be of no surprise that negative attachment representations are maintained and strengthened.[72]

Children who have an attachment disorder perceive themselves to be bad. As long as they perceive themselves to be bad, they will act bad. Acting bad produces a predictable response in others and confirms their belief system, which in an unhealthy sense is reassuring to the child who has an attachment disorder. It provides an element of stability and predictability to counter-balance their perception that their world is unpredictable and chaotic, this latter being anxiety evoking. Negative conduct also draws more attention than positive conduct. Consider the fact that newborn babies draw attention to their needs through affective displays that would later be considered to be antisocial. This behaviour, along with a gregarious smile, has emerged through evolution as an effective means by which the young child communicates with others and secures needs provision. It follows that children who are preoccupied with accessibility to needs provision are likely to use these infant strategies (i.e. charming smiles and screaming tantrums). We should not be surprised that these strategies are consistent with the two types of disorder of attachment referred to in this book.

In caring for children who have an attachment disorder, it is important to maintain a positive attitude and disposition towards the child as a person and not to be drawn into a perception of them as fundamentally bad because their behaviour is bad. Spending special time together and exclaiming over their positive qualities and abilities are useful starting points in this process, as is holding and maintaining positive thoughts about the child. Nevertheless, it is important to be mindful that in doing so you are acting unpredictably from the child's point of view. This will take some getting used to at first for the child and they may even actively resist (e.g. 'So you think I am good; well I'll show you just how bad I can be'). Nevertheless, in the longer term they will come to accept that you see them in a positive light and this will be the beginning of them seeing themselves the same way.

GLOSSARY OF TERMS

Aberrant: Behaviour that does not conform to societal standards and, as a result, damages relationships with others.

Accessibility: Having ready, easy, reliable and consistent access to basic human needs from an adult or adults who is/are in a caregiving role.

Adaptation: Being able to live successfully in one's social environment.

Affect: Emotion.

Affective attunement: Emotional connectedness, where two people express, and otherwise appear to experience, the same or similar emotion as each other.

Affect regulation: The capacity to control intensity of emotions for one's own benefit and in order to conform to conventional standards of emotional expression.

Anxiety: A pervasive feeling of worry or uneasiness, accompanied by physiological symptoms (e.g. sweating, palpitations, restlessness) and usually associated with an exaggerated perception of threat or danger.

Arousal: In this book, 'arousal' is used to refer to rate of brain activity.

Attachment: A term used to describe the dependency relationship a child develops towards his or her primary caregivers.

Attachment figure: Someone who provides physical and emotional care, has continuity and consistency in the child's life and has an emotional investment in the child's life.[73]

Attachment representations: The beliefs one has about self, others and interpersonal relationships.

Attributions: Beliefs – in this book, used to denote beliefs one has about self, others and interpersonal relationships.

Attunement experience: See affective attunement.

Bond: A uniting force that links people to one another.

Cognitive-behavioural therapy: A treatment methodology that is based on theories of cognition and learning and the remediation of thoughts and behaviours that precipitate and maintain maladjustment.

Compulsion: A seemingly irresistible act performed in response to an impulse. In the context of this book, the impulse is to obtain reassurance regarding accessibility to needs provision.

Dependency: Relying on others to sensitively, accurately and reliably respond to your needs and reasonable wishes.

Detached: The absence of emotional connectedness and dependency upon others.

Developmental delay: Refers to a condition whereby the development of an infant or child is slower than is normally expected.

Developmental milestone: Skills and abilities that most children learn at a certain age.

Developmental psychology: The scientific study of how children develop, including fine and gross motor development, language development, emotional development, social development, moral development and cognitive development.

Diagnosis: The process of categorising behaviour through evaluation of a person's history, presentation, the person's own reports concerning their behaviour and the reports of others who know them.

Dissociation: A process by which a person becomes detached from their immediate environment. A defence that develops in response to intolerably high levels of stress.

Empathy: A feeling of emotional connectedness to another, such that one feels the same or similar emotion and intensity of emotion.

Empirical evidence: Refers to knowledge or information that is gathered through scientific study.

Evolutionary: Used to refer to behaviour that has been selected through history, as it serves a useful purpose in the survival of the species.

Hypervigilance: Being acutely aware of one's surroundings, particularly for signs of threat or danger.

Infants: Children 0–2 years of age.

Insecure attachment: An outcome whereby an infant has either failed to learn that he or she can consistently depend upon their primary caregiver(s) to love, nurture and protect them, or has learnt that he or she cannot consistently depend upon their primary caregiver(s) to love, nurture and protect them.

Interactive repair: An action on the part of a caregiver adult whereby they positively reconnect with a dependent child in association with having had to admonish the child or otherwise discipline them from engaging in inappropriate behaviour or affective displays.

Maladaptive: Beliefs, behaviours and affective displays that compromise the person's success in living in their environment.

Motor development: The development of the capacity to roll, sit, crawl, walk, run, climb, jump, grasp and physically manipulate.

Naturalistic observation: Involves observing the subject in its natural environment as unobtrusively as possible.

Primary attachment relationships: The attachment relationships the child has with his or her main caregivers.

Primary dependency relationships: The relationship(s) between the infants and the person or persons who are their primary caregivers.

Psychoanalytic: Refers to a theory of personality, developed by Sigmund Freud, which focuses on the idea that human behaviour is governed by unconscious forces and repression of internal conflicts.

Psychoeducation: A process by which people are informed about psychological theories or other psychological information relevant to a mental disorder or condition and its treatment. Psychoeducation can be delivered verbally in the context of face-to-face interactions with a mental health professional and in the form of written information (also known as Bibliotherapy).

Psychological: To do with the mind.

Psychology: The science of the mind or mental life.

Psychotherapy: The use of psychological theories and methods in the treatment of mental disorders.

Secure attachment: An outcome whereby an infant has learnt that he or she can consistently depend upon their primary caregiver(s) to love, nurture and protect them.

Socialisation: The process of learning about the culture of one's social world and how to live in accordance with it.

Startle response: A physical, emotional and cognitive response to an unexpected event, such as a flash of light or a loud noise, whereby the infant reacts with sudden movements of the arms and legs, blinking and, in some instances, emotional distress.

Stranger reaction: Usually observed in infants and young children, it is recognised in the child seeking closeness or otherwise orienting to their primary attachment figures in the presence of a person who is relatively unknown to them. The classic sign of the stranger reaction is when young children stand slightly behind and cling to their parent's leg while shyly gazing at a relatively unknown person.

Therapeutic alliance: The creation of a particular relationship between the mental health professional and their patient that is specifically boundaried in order to ensure that the work of psychotherapy can be carried out effectively.

Trauma: An emotional or psychological injury, usually resulting from an extremely stressful or upsetting life experience.

ABOUT THE AUTHOR

Colby Pearce is the Principal Clinical Psychologist at Secure Start, an independent psychology practice in Adelaide, South Australia, that provides psychology services to children, adolescents and families. A graduate of the University of Adelaide, he was first registered to practise as a psychologist in 1995. His work since registration has incorporated the provision of assessment and psychotherapy services in the areas of child protection, family law, intercountry adoption, refugees and community child and family psychology. He holds, or has held, a number of appointments concerning the regulation of the psychology profession in Australia and is currently a member of the NT/SA/WA Regional Board of the Psychology Board of Australia. He was the founder and Director of the Child Wellbeing Clinics, Master of Psychology training clinics that operated between 2006 and 2008 as a joint initiative between the University of South Australia and Families SA and which provided a psychology service to children recovering from abuse, neglect and complex family trauma.

Colby has extensive experience in the teaching and training of psychologists and is the author of published articles that span such diverse topics as therapeutic foster care, promoting resilience in children and adolescent mental health. His 1994 publication *Predicting Suicide Attempts Among Adolescents* contributed to the assessment framework in an Australia-wide General Practitioner education and awareness programme concerning adolescent suicidality. Colby is also the author of a sister title *A Short Introduction to Promoting Resilience in Children*[74] and a therapeutic care programme called the Triple-A Model of Therapeutic Care. He is regularly called upon to speak about the care and management of children. He is married with three children of his own.

NOTES

1. Bowlby, J. (1969) *Attachment and Loss. Volume I: Attachment.* New York: Basic Books.

2. Ainsworth, M., Blehar, M., Waters, E. and Wall, S. (1978) *Patterns of Attachment: A Psychological Study of the Strange Situation.* New Jersey: Laurence Erlbaum and Associates.

3. Howes, C. (1999) 'Attachment Relationships in the Context of Multiple Caregivers.' In J. Cassidy and P. R. Shaver (eds). *Handbook of Attachment: Theory, Research and Clinical Applications* (pp.671–687). New York: The Guilford Press.

4. Howes, C. (1999) 'Attachment relationships in the context of multiple caregivers.' In J. Cassidy & P. R. Shaver (eds). *Handbook of attachment: Theory, research and clinical applications* (pp. 671–687). New York: The Guilford Press.

5. Bretherton, I. (1992) 'The origins of attachment theory: John Bowlby and Mary Ainsworth.' *Developmental Psychology 28*, 759–775.

6. Harlow, H. F. (1958) 'The nature of love.' *American Psychologist 13*, 673–685.

7. Ainsworth, M., Blehar, M., Waters, E. and Wall, S. (1978) *Patterns of Attachment: A Psychological Study of the Strange Situation.* New Jersey: Laurence Erlbaum and Associates.

8. Bowlby, J. (1969) *Attachment and Loss. Volume I: Attachment.* New York: Basic Books.

9. Bowlby, J. (1973) *Attachment and Loss. Volume I: Separation.* New York: Basic Books.

10. Ainsworth, M., Blehar, M., Waters, E. and Wall, S. (1978) *Patterns of Attachment: A Psychological Study of the Strange Situation.* New Jersey: Laurence Erlbaum and Associates.

11. Delaney, R. J. (2006) *Fostering Changes: Myth, Meaning and Magic Bullets in Attachment Theory.* Oklahoma: Wood 'N' Barnes.

12. Bowlby, J. (1969) *Attachment and Loss. Volume I: Attachment.* New York: Basic Books.

13. Bowlby, J. (1982) 'Attachment and Loss: Retrospect and Prospect.' *American Journal of Orthopsychiatry 52,* 4, 664–678.

14. Ainsworth, M., Blehar, M., Waters, E. and Wall, S. (1978) *Patterns of Attachment: A Psychological Study of the Strange Situation.* New Jersey: Laurence Erlbaum and Associates.

15. Delaney, R. J. (2006) *Fostering Changes: Myth, Meaning and Magic Bullets in Attachment Theory.* Oklahoma: Wood 'N' Barnes.

16. Ainsworth, M., Blehar, M., Waters, E. and Wall, S. (1978) *Patterns of Attachment: A Psychological Study of the Strange Situation.* New Jersey: Laurence Erlbaum and Associates.

17. Ainsworth, M., Blehar, M., Waters, E. and Wall, S. (1978) *Patterns of Attachment: A Psychological Study of the Strange Situation.* New Jersey: Laurence Erlbaum and Associates.

18. Erikson, E. (1950) *Children and Society.* New York: Norton.

19. Prior, V. and Glader, D. (2006) *Understanding Attachment and Attachment Disorders: Theory, Evidence and Practice.* London: Jessica Kingsley Publishers,

20. Ainsworth, M., Blehar, M., Waters, E. and Wall, S. (1978) *Patterns of Attachment: A Psychological Study of the Strange Situation.* New Jersey: Laurence Erlbaum and Associates.

21. Ainsworth, M., Blehar, M., Waters, E. and Wall, S. (1978) *Patterns of Attachment: A Psychological Study of the Strange Situation.* New Jersey: Laurence Erlbaum and Associates.

22. Main, M. and Solomon, J. (1990) 'Procedures for identifying infants as disorganised/disoriented during Ainsworth strange situations.' In M. T. Greenberg, D. Cicchetti and E. M. Cummings (eds) *Attachment in the Pre-school Years: Theory, Research and Intervention* (pp.121–160). Chicago: University of Chicago Press.

23. Skinner, B. F. (1948) 'Superstition in the pigeon.' *Journal of Experimental Psychology 38,* 168–172.

24. Skinner, B. F. (1938) The *Behavior of Organisms: An Experimental Analysis.* New York: Appleton-Century.

25. Ferster, C. B. and Skinner, B. F. (1957) *Schedules of Reinforcement.* New York: Appleton-Century-Crofts.

26. Delaney, R. J. (2006) *Fostering Changes: Myth, Meaning and Magic Bullets in Attachment Theory.* Oklahoma: Wood 'N' Barnes.

27. Bower, T. G. R. (1967) 'The development of object-permanence: Some studies of existence constancy.' *Perception and Psychophysics 2,* 9, 411–418.

28. Piaget, J. (1954) *The Construction of Reality in the Child.* New York: Basic Books.

29. Delaney, R. J. (2006) *Fostering Changes: Myth, Meaning and Magic Bullets in Attachment Theory*. Oklahoma: Wood 'N' Barnes.

30. Reite, M. and Fields, T. (eds) (1985) *The Psychobiology of Attachment and Separation*. Florida: Academic Press.

31. Livingstone, S. R. and Thompson, W. F. (2009) 'The emergence of music from theory of mind.' Musicae Scientae, Special Issue 2009–2010, 83–115.

32. Tronick, E., Heidelise, A., Adamson, L., Wise, S. and Berry Brazilton, T. (1978) 'The Infant's Response to Entrapment Between Contradictory Messages in Face-to-face Interaction.' *Journal of the American Academy of Child Psychiatry 17*, 1, 1–13.

33. Bowlby, J. (1969) *Attachment and Loss. Volume I: Attachment*. New York: Basic Books.

34. Erikson, E. (1950) *Childhood and Society*. New York: Norton.

35. Howes, Hamilton and Althusen (in press), cited by Howes, C. (1999) 'Attachment Relationships in the Context of Multiple Caregivers.' In J. Cassidy and P. R. Shaver (eds). *Handbook of Attachment: Theory, Research and Clinical Applications* (pp.671–687). New York: The Guilford Press.

36. Note: At five months of age a child is beginning to discriminate between familiar and unfamiliar adults but has yet to form an attachment to anyone.

37. American Psychiatric Association (2013) Diagnostic and Statistical Manual of Mental Disorders (5th ed.). Washington, DC: American Psychiatric Association.

38. Bowlby, J. (1973) *Attachment and Loss. Volume I: Separation*. New York: Basic Books.

39. Bowlby, J. (1973) *Attachment and Loss. Volume II: Separation: Anger and Anxiety*. New York: Basic Books.

40. Bowlby, J. (1980) *Attachment and Loss. Volume III: Loss: Sadness and Depression*. New York: Basic Books.

41. Bretherton, I. (1992) 'The origins of attachment theory: John Bowlby and Mary Ainsworth.' *Developmental Psychology 28*, 759–775.

42. Crowell, J. A., Treboux, D. and Waters, E. (2002) 'Stability of attachment representations: The transition to marriage.' *Developmental Psychology 38*, 4, 467–479.

43. Delaney, R. J. (2006) *Fostering Changes: Myth, Meaning and Magic Bullets in Attachment Theory*. Oklahoma: Wood 'N' Barnes.

44. Erikson, E. (1950) *Children and Society*. New York: Norton.

45. Delaney, R. J. (2006) *Fostering Changes: Myth, Meaning and Magic Bullets in Attachment Theory*. Oklahoma: Wood 'N' Barnes.

46. Bretherton, I., Ridgeway, D. and Cassidy, J. (1990) 'Assessing Internal Working Models of the Attachment Relationship: An Attachment Story Completion Task for 3-year-olds.' In M. T. Greenberg, D. Cicchetti and E. M. Cummings (eds) *Attachment in the Pre-school Years: Theory, Research and Intervention* (pp.273–308). Chicago: University of Chicago Press.

47. Speltz, M. (1990) 'The Treatment of Preschool Conduct Problems: An Integration of Behavioural and Attachment Concepts.' In M. T. Greenberg, D. Cicchetti and E. M. Cummings (eds) *Attachment in the Pre-school Years: Theory, Research and Intervention* (pp.399–426). Chicago: University of Chicago Press.

48. Aber, J. L., Allen, J. P., Carlson, V. and Cicchetti, D. (1989) 'The effects of maltreatment on development during early childhood: Recent studies and their theoretical, clinical, and policy implications.' In V. Carlson and D. Cicchetti (eds) *Child Maltreatment: Theory and Research on the Causes and Consequences of Child Abuse and Neglect* (pp.579– 619). New York: Cambridge University Press.

49. Delaney, R. J. (2006) *Fostering Changes: Myth, Meaning and Magic Bullets in Attachment Theory.* Oklahoma: Wood 'N' Barnes.

50. Main, M. (1996) 'Introduction to the special section on attachment and psychopathology: 2. Overview of the field of attachment.' *Journal of Consulting and Clinical Psychology 64,* 2, 237–243.

51. Palmer, A. (2012) 'What's the difference between these two brains?' *The Telegraph.* Available at: www.telegraph.co.uk/news/health/children/9637682/Whats-the-difference-between-these-two-brains.html, accessed on 8 August 2016.

52. Evidence for a faster idle speed is reflected in the disturbed sleeping patterns of children who have an attachment disorder. They struggle to wind down to go to sleep, they sleep less and their sleep is commonly reported as not being restful.

53. Delaney, R. (1994) *Fostering Changes: Treating Attachment-disordered Foster Children.* Colorado: Corbett.

54. Hughes, D. A. (1997) *Facilitating Developmental Attachment: The Road to Recovery and Behavioural Change in Foster and Adopted Children.* New Jersey: Jason Aronson Inc.

55. Bowlby, J. (1969) *Attachment and Loss. Volume I: Attachment.* New York: Basic Books.

56. Bowlby, J. (1973) *Attachment and Loss. Volume II: Separation: Anger and Anxiety.* New York: Basic Books.

57. Bowlby, J. (1980) *Attachment and Loss. Volume III: Loss: Sadness and Depression.* New York: Basic Books.

58. Bretherton, I. (1992) 'The origins of attachment theory: John Bowlby and Mary Ainsworth.' *Developmental Psychology 28,* 759–775.

59. Crowell, J. A., Treboux, D. and Waters, E. (2002) 'Stability of attachment representations: The transition to marriage.' *Developmental Psychology 38*, 4, 467–479.

60. Pearce, C. and Gibson, J. (2016) 'A preliminary evaluation of the Triple-A Model of Therapeutic Care in Donegal.' *Foster 2*, 94–104.

61. A form of punishment whereby a child is temporarily sent to a place where they are excluded from interaction with others, usually for the same number of minutes as their chronological age. It is not particularly useful for children who have an attachment disorder, as we want them to be more connected with the family. Rather, use 'time-in', a form of discipline where the consequence involves having to perform a chore or some other undesirable activity with their caregiver.

62. Perry, B. D., Pollard, R. A., Blakley, T. L., Baker, W. L. and Vigilante, D. (1995) 'Childhood trauma, the neurobiology of adaptation, and "use-dependent" development of the brain: How "states" become "traits".' *Infant Mental Health Journal 16*, 4, 271–289.

63. www.securestart.com.au

64. Ritchie, S. A. (1996) 'Attachment relationships of substance-exposed children with their caregivers and their teachers.' *Dissertation Abstracts International 56*, 10-A, 3892A.

65. Schwartz, E. and Davis, A. S. (2006) 'Reactive attachment disorder: Implications for school readiness and school functioning.' *Psychology in the Schools 43*, 4, 471–479.

66. Shonk, S. M. and Cicchetti, D. (2001) 'Maltreatment, competency deficits, and risk for academic and behavioral maladjustment.' *Developmental Psychology 37*, 3–17.

67. Crittenden, P. M. (1992) 'Quality of attachment in the preschool years.' *Development and Psychopathology 4*, 209–241.

68. Schore, A. (1994) *Affect Regulation and the Origin of Self: The Neurobiology of Emotional Development.* New Jersey: Earlbaum.

69. Jernberg, A. M. and Booth, P. B. (2001) *Theraplay: Helping Parents and Children Build Better Relationships Through Attachment-based* Play (2nd ed.). San Francisco: Jossey Bass.

70. Cook, W. C. and Douglas, E. M. (1998) 'The looking glass self in family context: A social relations analysis.' *Journal of Family Psychology 12*, 3, 299–309.

71. Yeung, K. T. and Martin, J. L. (2003) 'The looking glass self: An empirical test and elaboration.' *Social Forces 81*, 3, 843–879

72. Pearce, C. M. (2010) 'An integration of theory, science and reflective clinical practice in the care and management of attachment-disordered children: A Triple A approach.' *Educational and Child Psychology (Special Issue on Attachment) 27*, 3, 73–86.

73. Howes, Hamilton and Althusen (in press), cited by Howes, C. (1999) 'Attachment Relationships in the Context of Multiple Caregivers'. In J. Cassidy and P. R. Shaver (eds). *Handbook of Attachment: Theory, Research and Clinical Applications* (pp.671–687). New York: The Guilford Press.

74. Pearce, C. (2011) *A Short Introduction to Promoting Resilience in Children.* London and Philadelphia: Jessica Kingsley Publishers.

INDEX